KNOWING THE TRINITY

Knowing the Trinity

Practical Thoughts for Daily Life

Ryan M. McGraw

ALLIANCE®
OF CONFESSING EVANGELICALS
600 Eden Road • Lancaster • Pennsylvania 17601

The Alliance of Confessing Evangelicals
600 Eden Road
Lancaster, PA 17601
215-546-3696 / Fax 215-735-5133
orders@alliancenet.org
AllianceNet.org

Printed in the United States of America

ISBN 978-0-9980102-9-8

The purpose of Meet the Puritans is to introduce the theology and piety of the seventeenth century English Puritans in particular and of sixteenth–eighteenth century Reformed orthodoxy in general.

Our audience is threefold: first, Reformed Christians who need to reconnect with their heritage; second, evangelical Christians who need to be introduced to this heritage; and third, the world that needs the answer this heritage gives.

Our goals in doing this are instruction concerning "the unsearchable riches of Christ" (Ephesians 3:8) found in the writings of the 16th–18th centuries so that a new generation would be filled with love for Christ and His historic church so that it might serve Him in the world more effectively.

With this in mind we present to you this resource.

For more resources, we encourage you to visit our website at-MeetthePuritans.org, a ministry of the Alliance of Confessing Evangelicals.

To Decherd and Sylvia Stevens

Parents by marriage and a father and a mother in the Lord.

Contents

Foreword

The Reformation-era *Belgic Confession of Faith* (1561) said of the doctrine of the Holy Trinity, "although this doctrine surpasses human understanding, we nevertheless believe it now, through the Word, waiting to know and enjoy it fully in heaven" (Article 9). Our full knowledge and enjoyment of our God as Father, Son, and Holy Spirit will be in eternity; but there is a knowledge and enjoyment of it now in this life. What the *Belgic Confession* implied, John Owen made explicit in his *Of Communion with God the Father, Son, and Holy Ghost, each Person Distinctly, in Love, Grace, and Consolation; or, The Saints' Fellowship with the Father, Son, and Holy Ghost Unfolded* (1657). In *Communion*, Owen said 'there is no grace whereby our souls go forth unto God, no act of divine worship yielded unto Him, no duty or obedience performed, but they are distinctly directed unto Father, Son, and Spirit.'[1] In other words, everything we do in relationship to our God is related to Him as Triune. The reality, though, is that we hardly think of the Trinity except merely as a doctrine we affirm against false theologies.

This is where Ryan McGraw's work is so helpful. Following in the tradition of Owen, he seeks to explain and apply God as Triune for all of our lives: how we think, how we speak, and how we act. The Trinity is not just the structural background of Christian theology it is the substance of living out Christian faith, hope, and love in relationship with the one true God and with each Person in particular as Father, Son, and Holy Spirit.

Rev. Daniel R. Hyde

[1] *The Works of John Owen*, ed. William H. Goold (Edinburgh: The Banner of Truth Trust, fifth printing 1997), 2:15.

Preface

In his book, *Knowing Christ*, Mark Jones noted that a "rich Trinitarian theology…needs to be reignited in the life of the Church."[2] Mark highlights something that continues to strike a chord with me: *The Triune God is what makes the Christian faith and life worth believing and living*. Yet I find that few Christians recognize the rich Trinitarian contours of Scripture, especially of the New Testament. Even fewer regard the doctrine of the Trinity as devotional. This brings me to the purpose of this book: I want to teach believers how to love the Triune God better by bringing the Trinitarian background of Scripture to the foreground. This book focuses on the "triadic" passages in the New Testament, which refer to all three Persons of the Trinity.

The English Puritan John Owen (1616-1683) first opened my eyes to such triadic passages. When invited to preach at the Puritan Reformed Theological Seminary conference in 2012, I chose Ephesians 2:18 as my text ("Through Him, we both have access to the Father, by one Spirit"), which was also one of Owen's favorite passages.[3] Every time I have preached this sermon since then, I have received the same reaction. Most people had never seen the Trinity behind so many teachings in the Bible. Once they do, they testify that the Gospel comes to life in ways that they had never imagined. Many have asked me over the past four years to put some of my reflections on the Trinity to writing. This work represents a prayerful attempt to fulfill these requests.

In the chapters that follow, I will lay the foundation for Trinitar-

---

[2] Mark Jones, *Knowing Christ* (Edinburgh: Banner of Truth, 2015), 79.

[3] The written byproduct of this sermon appears in Ryan M. McGraw, "The Need for a Trinitarian Piety (Eph. 2:18)," in *The Beauty and Glory of the Father*, ed. Joel R. Beeke (Grand Rapids: Reformation Heritage Books, 2013), 141–53.

ian piety by looking at the saving work of each divine Person—Father, Son, and Holy Spirit. The last chapter summarizes the themes of the entire book in light of the Trinitarian blessing in 2 Corinthians 13:14. The study questions at the end of each chapter are designed to promote practical group discussion in order to make the material stick better. The list of triadic passages in Scripture at the end of the book is meant to help readers meditate on the glories of the Triune God in broader connections than the verses cited in individual chapters.

My aim is that believers will recover the "rich Trinitarian theology" of the New Testament that will lead to devotion to the Triune God. As Joel Beeke once told me, people are more likely to read several short books than one long one. The Lord has used this book to promote this goal in my family, in my former congregation, and in myself. My earnest prayer is that He would so use it in the lives of as many others whose hearts He is pleased to stir up to read this book.

Ryan M. McGraw

Acknowledgements

I thank the Triune God for directing me to John Owen, who first led me by the hand to meditate on the themes presented in this book. His Communion with God changed my thought and life second only to my first conversion to Christ. My prayer is that the Lord would help me pass on in some measure to others what Owen passed along to me.

I am grateful to the congregations of Grace Presbyterian Church (Conway, SC) and First Orthodox Presbyterian Church (Sunnyvale, CA) for receiving and responding positively to the sermons I preached on most of the texts in this volume. One of the greatest joys of my ministry in both of these congregations was preaching to people who were eager to behold the glory of God in the face of Jesus Christ. If I have left a legacy with you, then may the Spirit grant that it consists primarily in increasing your love for the Triune God.

Thank you to my many Facebook friends who helped me narrow the title to Knowing the Trinity. Thanks to Clay Woody, Vernon Shoaf, and my wife, Krista, for reworking the subtitle and preventing me from going into Puritan blockhead mode in naming my books.

Adam Harris also saved me much time by preparing the appendix to the book and improving readability. Thank you, brother, for being a good student and a good friend in the Lord and for helping me bring this book to print.

Danny Hyde and Bob Brady are the primary culprits for pushing this project to the press. Bob's enthusiasm and excitement over this book have encouraged me in the Lord from beginning to end. Danny deserves credit for the final order of the chapters and improving readability and who sympathizes with a fellow Californian living as a missionary in a foreign land.

Family worship has been the crucible in which I tested the usefulness and simplicity of the ideas in this book. My wife and children have been enthusiastic and prayerful supporters of my labors to promote the glory of the Triune God, both in my academic and pastoral work. It is a joy to have our household as part the Father's household, for our family to belong to Christ's body, and for us to receive the Spirit who is building us into a holy temple to God with His people.

May the Lord bless this book to refresh many souls and may the joy of the Lord increase in all who helped make these labors possible.

Ryan M. McGraw
Professor of Systematic Theology
Greenville Presbyterian Theological Seminary
Adjunct Professor of Doctoral Studies
Puritan Reformed Theological Seminary
2016

INTRODUCTION

Chapter One

What Is Trinitarian Piety?

"Through Him, we both have access to the Father, by one Spirit" (Ephesians 2:18)

Have you ever wondered why the Trinity is an essential doctrine of the Christian faith? The Westminster Shorter Catechism directs us to stand in awe before God when it says, "God is a Spirit, infinite, eternal, and unchangeable, in His being, wisdom, power, holiness, justice, goodness, and truth" (Q&A 4). While we should be lost in wonder over the glories of this God, He is also personal and intrapersonal. The relationship that the Father, the Son, and the Holy Spirit hold to each other in eternity is the foundation of the relationship we hold to both God and fellow believers in time. The attributes of God teach us what kind of God the Trinity is. The Persons of the Godhead provide us with a window into who God is and how He relates to His creatures. The Trinity defies our comprehension and we must avoid using analogies to explain it. Every analogy either reduces Him to one person who takes on three different roles, or to three individuals who do not possess the same undivided deity. However, even though God's Triunity transcends our comprehension, the apostle Paul placed this doctrine at the heart of our faith and of our Christian experience. Therefore, it is to our detriment if we do not think about our Christian lives in terms of fellowship with the work of all three divine Persons. The Triune God Himself is our comfort, our blessedness, and our exceedingly great reward.

The term "piety" describes a fundamental quality of personal holiness. Piety refers to a disposition of the heart that should permeate all that we think, do, and say as believers.[4] Piety reflects our Chris-

---

[4] Richard Muller defines *pietas* as, "the personal confidence in, reverence for, and fear of God that conduces to true worship of and devotion to God." Richard A. Muller, *Dictionary of Latin and Greek Theological Terms: Drawn Principally from Protestant Scholastic Theology* (Grand Rapids, MI: Baker Book House, 1985), 228.

tian experience and the devotion of our hearts to God. It is rooted in fellowship with God as it relates to how we live to God and for His glory. Piety is a fountain that is filled through fellowship with God and that overflows into every area of life. It involves the renovation of the entire person into what the Bible calls "the image of God" (Eph. 4:25; Col. 3:10). It is the reservoir from which we draw waters from the well of salvation in Christ.

In Ephesians 2:18, the apostle Paul places all three Persons of the Godhead at the center of our relationship to God and to fellow believers. In addition to this, Paul establishes the proper order in which God approaches us and in which we approach Him. We come to the Father, through the Son, by the Spirit. Conversely, the Father comes to us through His Son and by the Spirit. The Father planned our redemption, the Son purchased our redemption, and the Spirit applies our redemption (Eph. 1:3-14). We walk in peace and in unity with God and with one another in Christ (Eph. 2:14) by depending upon the Spirit, coming through the Son, and resting on the Father as the great object of our worship and hope. As the being of God is both one and many, so, in the Church, believers are both one in Christ even while they fulfill diverse functions (Eph. 4:1-7). In this way, Paul summarized the entirety of our relation to God as well as to fellow believers in terms of the doctrine of the Trinity. By doing so, he placed what is perhaps the deepest doctrine of the Christian faith at the heart and center of the Christian life. As the Puritan, Thomas Manton (1620–1677), noted, "We were made for understanding this mystery."[5] As he wrote in relation to expressing unity and diversity among believers, "Let us study to imitate the Trinity."[6]

We need a Trinitarian piety because we have a Trinitarian faith. Just as a student in medical school does not truly know his field until he operates on real patients, so we do not begin adequately to grasp God's Triunity until we know Him by experience. *The Belgic Confession of Faith* describes the consummation of this experience when it states, "And although this doctrine far surpasses all human understanding, nevertheless, we now believe it by means of the Word of

---

[5] Thomas Manton, *The Complete Works* (London: Nisbet, 1870), 11:102.

[6] Manton, *Works*, 11:333.

God, but expect hereafter to enjoy the perfect knowledge and benefit thereof in Heaven" (Article 9). The Church increasingly uses confused expressions in relation to the Trinity because Her members have little practical use for such a complex doctrine. However, our Reformed forefathers argued that the Trinity was the most practical and important doctrine of all. For example, the Congregational Savoy Declaration of Faith (1658) says, "[the] doctrine of the Trinity is the foundation of all our communion with God, and comfortable dependence upon Him."[7] Similarly, the Dutch theologian, Gisbertus Voetius (1589–1676), called the Trinity the foundation of fundamentals,[8] adding that every article of the faith is married to this doctrine.[9] Johannes Hoornbeeck (1617–1666) observed that we know the Persons of the Godhead better by experiencing Their saving work in our lives than we do by man-made analogies.[10] Ephesians 2:18 provides a window through which we gain glimpses of the biblical foundations of such statements.

If we lose the usefulness of the doctrine of the Trinity, then we will likely lose the doctrine itself. If we worship the being of God, but we neglect the Persons of the Godhead, then we run the risk of turning the true God into an idol and forsaking the entire foundation of the Christian faith. As William Perkins (1558–1602) once wrote, "when the Godhead is abstracted from the Father, Son, and Holy Ghost, God is transformed into an idol... And the unity of the Godhead is to be adored in the Trinity of persons."[11] This means, as James Durham (1622–1658) observed, "Although there be three persons in the glorious Godhead, and all are to be worshiped; yet

---

[7] *Savoy Declaration*, 2.3. This paragraph is adapted from my forthcoming booklet, *Is the Trinity Practical?* This booklet is based on an extended exposition and application of Ephesians 2:18 in the broader context of Ephesians.

[8] *fundamentum fundamenti*

[9] Gisperti Voetii, *Selectarum Disputationum Theologicarum, Pars Prima* (Utrecht, 1648). 472, 478.

[10] Johannes Hoornbeeck (1617-1666), *Theologiae Practicae* (Utrecht, 1663), 1:136.

[11] William Perkins, *A Warning Against the Idolatrie of the Last Times and an Instruction Touching Religious, or Diuine Worship.* ([Cambridge]: Printed by Iohn Legat, printer to the Vniuersitie of Cambridge. And are to be sold at the signe of the Crowne in Pauls Churchyard [London], by Simon Waterson, 1601), 3.

there are not three objects of worship...Though the three persons be really distinct from each other; yet none of them is really distinct from the essence of the Godhead."[12] The doctrine of the Trinity is necessary because we cannot explain the Gospel apart from it, and God designed the Christian life to flow from this doctrine as waters from a fountain. The glory of God is the goal of your salvation, yet the glory that God seeks in your salvation goes to all three persons in the Godhead.

Let us seek to develop a self-consciously Trinitarian piety. The chapters below aim to furnish you with the tools needed to build a Trinitarian faith, to cultivate a Trinitarian piety, and to live a godly life in fellowship with the Triune God.

Study Questions:

1.What is "piety" and why is it important?

2.How does Paul use the doctrine of the Trinity in Ephesians 2:18? What does this teach you about the Gospel and the Christian life?

3.Why is the practical application of the doctrine of the Trinity necessary to preserve the doctrine of the Trinity?

4.What are some ways in which you can cultivate a Trinitarian piety?

---

[12] James Durham, *A Commentarie Upon the Book of the Revelation Wherein the Text Is Explained, the Series of the Several Prophecies Contained in That Book, Deduced.the Periods and Succession of Times At, or About Which, These Prophecies Began to Be and Those That Are yet to Be Fulfilled: Together with Some Practical Observations, and Several Digressions: Delivered in Several Lectures* (London: Printed for the Company of Stationers, 1658), 11.

Chapter Two
The Trinity in the New Testament

The Trinity is the canvas on which the teachings of the New Testament are painted. The apostles did not try to prove the doctrine of the Trinity. The greatest proof of the doctrine of the Trinity is that the authors of the New Testament could hardly explain the Gospel without it.[13] The rest of this book will show from various passages how and why this is true. Unlike a canvas, however, the Trinity should not remain in the background of our thinking. It must come to the foreground in order to bring out the beauty of the New Testament painting of Christian faith and life.

We cannot prove the Trinity from a single passage of Scripture. This means that this chapter differs from the rest of this book. As we proceed to prove the doctrine, we should remember, as Thomas Watson (1620–1686) wrote, "Our narrow thoughts can no more comprehend the Trinity in unity, than a little nutshell can hold all the water of the sea."[14] The preceding chapter highlighted the need for a Trinitarian piety. This chapter lays the foundation, briefly, for Trinitarian doctrine. The doctrine of the Trinity grows out of a series of questions that seek to do justice to the entire teaching of the New Testament. It is important for you to have the answers to

---

[13] Robert Letham, *The Holy Trinity: In Scripture, History, Theology, and Worship* (Phillipsburg, NJ: P & R Pub., 2004), chapter 3.

[14] Thomas Watson, *A Body of Practical Divinity, Consisting of Above One Hundred Seventy Six Sermons on the Lesser Catechism Composed by the Reverend Assembly of Divines at Westminster: With a Supplement of Some Sermons on Several Texts of Scripture. by Thomas Watson, Formerly Minister at St. Stephen's Walbrook, London. Printed from His Own Hand-Writing. Recommended by Several Ministers to Masters of Families and Others.* (London: printed for Thomas Parkurst, at the Bible and Three Crowns in Cheapside, near Mercers-Chappel, 1692), 62.

these at your fingertips as you witness to others and as you navigate prayerfully through the Bible. As Robert Letham observes, "It is my belief that a recovery of the Trinity at the ground level, the level of the ordinary minister and believer, will help revitalize the life of the Church and, in turn, its witness to the world."[15] Our working definition for the Trinity is, "There are three persons in the Godhead; the Father, the Son, and the Holy Ghost; and these three are one God, the same in substance, equal in power and glory."[16] Proofs for the Trinity proceed like building a pyramid of which the doctrine of the Trinity serves as the capstone.

God Is One

Proofs for the Trinity begin naturally with passages relating to the unity of God, since this is where the Old Testament begins. The Persons in the Godhead are revealed only gradually.[17] While some object to proceeding in this order, it is important to recognize that this is the order in which God revealed Himself. He declared that he was one (Deut. 6:4) and that there was no God besides Him (Deut. 32:39; Is. 43:11; 44:6; 45:5). Referring to false gods, Moses wrote, "For their rock is not like our Rock, even our enemies themselves being judges" (Deut. 32:31). Israel must have no other gods before Him (Ex. 20:3). The gods of the nations are idols that can neither hear, nor speak, nor answer, nor do good or evil (1 Chron. 16:25; Ps. 96:5; 115:3–8; 135:15–18). In Isaiah's extended satire against idolatry, he depicted people as foolish and blind when they cut down a tree, crafting one part into an idol to worship and burning the other part in the fire to warm themselves. (Is. 44:9–20). Paul described unbelievers as, "Professing to be wise, they became fools, and changed the glory of the incorruptible God into an image made like corruptible man—and birds and four-footed animals and creeping things" (Rom. 1:22–23). Rejecting God as the only true God and our God

[15] Letham, *The Holy Trinity*, 7.

[16] *Westminster Shorter Catechism*, question 6.

[17] "Person" in relation to the doctrine of the Trinity refers to the distinct personal subsistences of the Father, Son, and Holy Spirit. Person does not refer here, as it often does in contemporary language, to distinct individuals.

and Redeemer is the heart of idolatry.[18] This means that idolatry includes false philosophies, religions, and even atheism. The root of all of the sins that run rampant in our society is that people do not retain the true God in their thinking (Rom. 1:28). Paul went so far as describing all unbelievers, whether religious or not, as Atheists (Eph. 2:12; Greek: atheoi). The New Testament retains and assumes the Old Testament teaching that there is only one God (1 Cor. 8:6; etc.). This point prevents us from concluding that there are three gods instead of one in relation to the Trinity. We must forsake idols and worship the one true and living God (1 Thess. 1:9).

This One God Is Three

There are three Persons that the New Testament refers to as God. While there are hints of more than one divine Person in the Old Testament (Is. 48:16; Zech. 2:8–9; etc.), the New Testament alone makes clear what was previously obscure and vague.

The Father

We begin appropriately with the Father. The Father's deity is largely taken for granted in the New Testament. Most generic references to "God" refer to Him (e.g., John 17:3; 1 Cor. 8:6; etc.). He represents the majesty of the entire Godhead. This is why the Bible says things like, "For there is one God and one Mediator between God and men, the Man Christ Jesus" (1 Tim. 2:5). This does not mean that the Father is God to the exclusion of the Son, but rather that the Son is the only means by which we come to the Father (John 14:6), who represents the entire Trinity. You must know the only true God and Jesus Christ whom He has sent (John 17:3) because, "Whoever denies the Son does not have the Father either; he who acknowledges the Son has the Father also" (1 John 2:23).

The Son

The New Testament authors call the Son God explicitly at least twice (Rom. 9:5; 1 John 5:20) and the Spirit at least once (Acts 5:3–

---

[18] See *Westminster Shorter Catechism*, questions 44 and 46, which I have combined in this sentence.

4). However, this is not the only evidence for the Son's deity. The *Westminster Larger Catechism* 11 states helpfully, "The Scriptures manifest that the Son and the Holy Ghost are God equal with the Father, ascribing unto them such names, attributes, works, and worship, as are proper to God only." The Son has divine attributes, such as omniscience and omnipresence, as demonstrated when he "saw" Philip before he called him (Jn. 1:48). When Jesus said, "before Abraham was, I am," (John 8:58), the Pharisees recognized the intentional allusion to God's personal name, Yahweh, in Exodus 3:14 when they took up stones to execute Him for blasphemy (John 8:59; see Jn. 10:33). Christ also performed works, such as creating the world, that are ascribed in Scripture to God and that God alone can do (Heb. 1:8-12). Finally, Christ is the object of divine worship, both on earth (John 20:28; Matt. 28:17; Luke 24:52), and in heaven (Rev. 5:8-14). While Christ received the name Jesus at His birth (Matt. 1:21), He received the name Lord upon His ascension (Phil. 2:9). He who was born David's son was also David's Lord (Ps. 110:1; Matt. 22:44), and He was declared to be the Son of God with power by the resurrection of the dead (Rom. 1:4). It is no longer sufficient to confess that Yahweh is Lord. We must confess that Jesus is Lord, and thus Jesus is Yahweh. One day every knee will bow with every tongue confessing Jesus' true identity to the glory of God the Father (Phil. 2:9–11).

The Spirit

The Spirit is God equally with the Father and the Son. There is only one direct statement in the New Testament that proves the deity of the Spirit (Acts 5:3–5). Yet the catechism cited above furnishes us with abundant avenues through which to prove the Spirit's deity and personality. He has divine attributes as the one who searches our hearts (1 Cor. 2:10–12; Rom. 8:26–27). He does divine works, such as bringing order out of chaos in creation (Gen. 1:2), striving with men (Gen. 6:3), and sending forth Gospel overtures (Rev. 22:17). Accordingly, as we confess in the Nicene Creed, "together with the Father and the Son He is worshipped and glorified." We are baptized into His name, which is an act of worship (Matt. 28:19). The Spirit is not a divine force; He is a divine Person. He can be grieved and His influences can be quenched (Eph. 4:30; 1 Thess. 5:19).

These Three Are Distinct

We still do not have the full doctrine of the Trinity. Proving the unity of the Godhead and the divinity of the Persons is insufficient to establish the doctrine of the Trinity. It is necessary to show the distinction and relation between the Persons. John Calvin defined personhood in relation to the Trinity as "an incommunicable quality."[19] Personhood in the Trinity means that God does not put on masks by which He sometimes acts as the Father, and at other times as the Son or the Spirit. All three Persons were present at Christ's baptism and They are personally distinct (Matt. 3:16). Jesus, as a distinct person, prayed to His Father (John 11:41–42; 17; etc.). As the God man, Jesus obeyed His Father (Gal. 4:1–4; Phil. 2:5–8). The Father and the Son together send the Spirit to the Church (John 15:26; Acts 2:33). God is one being in three Persons. The divine Persons are not like three slices that make up a pie. As Francis Cheynell (1608–1665), wrote, "The single Godhead, the whole Godhead is in every single Person, and it is common to all three in a singular and glorious way."[20] How the Triune God acts in time reflects who He is in eternity. The Father begets the Son in eternity (without beginning or end) and the Spirit proceeds (eternally) from the Father and the Son. All three Persons work in every act of God, but in appropriate ways, reflecting their eternal order and relations. For example, redemption is from the Father, through the Son, by the Spirit (Eph. 1:3–14). As a result, we come to the Father, by one Spirit, through Christ (Eph. 2:18). This divine order and pattern applies to every divine work from creation, to Christ's incarnation, to the resurrection of the dead.

As Thomas Watson wrote, "The Trinity is purely an object of faith; the plumb–line of reason is too short to fathom this mystery,

---

[19] Cited in J. van Genderen and W. H Velema, *Concise Reformed Dogmatics*, ed. Gerrit Bilkes and Ed M Van der Maas (Phillipsburg, NJ: P&R Pub., 2008), 153.

[20] Francis Cheynell, *The Divine Trinunity of the Father, Son, and Holy Spirit, Or, the Blessed Doctrine of the Three Coessentiall Subsistents in the Eternall Godhead Without Any Confusion or Division of the Distinct Subsistences or Multiplication of the Most Single and Entire Godhead Acknowledged, Beleeved, Adored by Christians, in Opposition to Pagans, Jewes, Mahumetans, Blasphemous and Antichristian Hereticks, Who Say They Are Christians, but Are Not* (London: Printed by T.R. and E.M. for Samuel Gellibrand, 1650), 78.

but where reason cannot wade, there faith must swim."[21] The numerous components used here to formulate the doctrine of the Trinity reinforce how this doctrine functions in the New Testament. The Trinity is a thread that, if removed, would unravel the entire New Testament. The Trinity is the backdrop on which our Christian experience is painted. It is the capstone to the pyramid of faith. This brief sketch of the doctrine of the Trinity is like learning a language that you need to master in order to read your Bible well. Let us learn to understand the doctrine of the Trinity better so that we can learn to love the Triune God better.

Study Questions:

1. How should you respond to people who argue that the Trinity is a construction of the Church and that it is not found in Scripture?

2. Make a brief biblical case for the doctrine of the Trinity. What components are needed to give a complete case for the Trinity?

3. How is the Trinity related to the teaching of the New Testament? What would happen if we removed this doctrine from our faith?

[21] Watson, *A Body of Practical Divinity*, 64.

Chapter Three

The Trinity and the Plan of Salvation

"Peter, an apostle of Jesus Christ, to the strangers scattered throughout Pontus, Galatia, Cappadocia, Asia, and Bithynia, Elect according to the foreknowledge of God the Father, through sanctification of the Spirit, unto obedience and sprinkling of the blood of Jesus Christ: Grace unto you, and peace, be multiplied" (1 Peter 1:1–2)

These verses are like reading a summary of a great book. This summary describes the plan and purpose of the divine author of salvation, what His book is about, and how it ends. These verses unfold the story of redemption. Redemption begins with the Father's purpose of election. The story regards Christ, who purchased the Father's elect with His blood. It concludes with the Spirit, who sanctifies the elect through Christ's blood. The Spirit does this work in human history through calling people to faith in Christ and by making them holy. He perfects this work at the end of history, when the saints are made perfectly blessed in the full enjoyment of God to all eternity.[22] Subsequent chapters will show that this does not mean that all three divine Persons are not active in the Father's plan, the Son's purchase, and the Spirit's application of redemption. Rather, this passage unites the work of all three Persons in redemption by teaching us that the Spirit sanctifies the elect of God through applying Christ's blood to them. This picture provides us with a snapshot of the entire work of redemption. This gives us a platform from which to view the Gospel in Trinitarian terms.

The Father's Plan

Redemption fulfills the Father's eternal plan. Most Christians do not

[22] *Westminster Shorter Catechism*, question 38.

distinguish between election and predestination. However, election refers to God's choice of some people to salvation (Eph. 1:4), while predestination refers to the end for which He chose them (Eph. 1:5). God chose us to be His and He predestined us to adoption. Some speak as though only some Christians believe in predestination. However, everyone who takes the Bible seriously must have a view of election and predestination, because these are biblical terms. The elect in 1 Peter 1:1–2 were dispersed among the nations. They were those who were called from every tribe, tongue, people, and nation to be the Lord's people (Rev. 5:9). Though unknown to the world (1 John 3:1), they are known by God (Ps. 1:6; 1 Cor. 8:3), according to His foreknowledge (Rom. 8:29). God's foreknowledge here does not refer to God's looking down the corridors of time in order to see who would believe. It is God and not man who does the electing here. He did not choose the elect because of faith, but He chose them for faith and for salvation through faith in Christ. Acts 2:33 illustrates this by referring to God's foreknowledge as His "determinate counsel." God did not merely know that Christ would be crucified. He loved His own and sent His Son to die for them at the hands of wicked men (Matt. 1:21). Romans 8:29–30 depicts God's foreknowledge as a loving act that set in motion the entire chain of redemption accomplished and applied. Redemption is an act of the mercy of God alone (Rom. 9:18; Titus 3:5). The Bible does not present the doctrine of election in order to create logical complexities in our evangelism and personal lives, but to comfort those who believe in Christ. The Father's work in election and predestination should lead us to assurance of salvation and to praise His glorious grace (Eph. 1:6). If you trust in Christ, then you must love the Father who elected you according to His foreknowledge.

The Spirit's Application

The Spirit powerfully applies redemption. Peter moves from redemption planned to redemption applied under the word, "sanctification." God relates to us in covenant. Yet there is a compact between God and Christ before there is a compact between God and believers through Christ. As Patrick Gillespie (1617–1675) stated,

"The covenant made with us did spring out of the covenant made with Christ; and as is commonly distinguished, the covenant of reconciliation, whereby we are actually recovered and reconciled unto God, is bottomed upon the covenant of redemption."[23] The eternal covenant of redemption between the Father and the Son, with the consent of the Spirit, culminates in applying redemption to sinners in the covenant of grace. This is where Peter found the Christians to whom he wrote and this is where we find ourselves today. Being sanctified means being set apart as holy to the Lord (Ex. 19:10).

The Holy Spirit sanctifies believers in two ways. First, He does so through setting us apart from the world and the dominion of sin (Rom. 6:5–11; 1 Cor. 6:11). He does this through the new birth (1 John 5:19; 1 Peter 1:23). This is why the Bible calls believers saints, which means sanctified ones (1 Cor. 1:2; Ps. 16:3). This is probably what Peter meant in our text. Second, the Spirit sanctifies us through making us holy in practice as well. This is a gradual work of God in which we make progress until we enter into glory (2 Cor. 3:18). If the Father's foreknowledge and election begins the chain in Romans 8:29–30, then the Spirit holds the links of the chain together in an unbreakable series of events. In verse five, Peter says that believers are kept by the power of God through faith for salvation. We have been saved from the wrath to come (1 Thess. 1:10), but our salvation is "ready to be revealed at the last time." Salvation means more than being counted righteous in Christ. Salvation means being safe: in this life and in the next. As we sing in the hymn, Amazing Grace, "Twas grace that brought me safe thus far, and grace will lead me home." This is a work of the Spirit in particular. Persevere confidently in faith, knowing that the Spirit who sanctified you and who sanctifies you preserves you in faith for final salvation.

---

[23] Patrick Gillespie, *The Ark of the Covenant Opened, Or, a Treatise of the Covenant of Redemption Between God and Christ, as the Foundation of the Covenant of Grace the Second Part, Wherein Is Proved, That There Is Such a Covenant, the Necessity of It, the Nature, Properties, Parties Thereof, the Tenor, Articles, Subject-Matter of Redemption, the Commands, Conditions, and Promises Annexed, the Harmony of the Covenant of Reconciliation Made with Sinners, Wherein They Agree, Wherein They Differ, Grounds of Comfort from the Covenant of Suretiship* (London: Printed for Thomas Pankhurst, 1677), 1.

The Son's Purchase

Redemption is based on the Son's glorious purchase. The Person and work of the Son is the plot and the content of the biblical storyline. The Spirit sanctifies us "for obedience to Jesus Christ." We obey Christ first by believing in the Gospel (Heb. 3–4). We, in principle, believe whatever Christ says to us. Like Peter, we must confess that we have nowhere else to go, since Christ alone has the words of everlasting life (John 6:68). We must particularly trust in Him as the one who died for us and who rose again from the dead (1 Cor. 15:4). As a result of obeying Him through believing in Him, we must begin a life of obeying Him in everything else. God's adopted children must bear the family likeness. Without holiness, no one will see the Lord (Heb. 12:14). The Father chose us in Christ before time began that we might walk in good works in Christ, which He prepared beforehand (Eph. 2:10). Sprinkling was how the priests applied blood in the Old Testament (Heb. 9:21). The sprinkling of Christ's blood is the means by which the Spirit sanctifies us. As the blood of bulls and goats sanctified worshipers ceremonially under the Old Testament, so the blood of Christ sanctifies us actually by removing the guilt and power of our sins (Heb. 12:24). Christ makes a Christian. We know that we are elected by the Father and sanctified through the Spirit by our faith and obedience toward Christ. Do you believe whatever He tells you and are you willing to do whatever He commands you?

Trust in the Spirit to continue to sanctify you through the sprinkling of Christ's blood. In doing so, be assured of your election by the Father and of your sprinkling with Christ's blood.

Study Questions:

1. How does 1 Peter 1:1–2 give us hints at God's eternal plan in redemption?
2. What is the difference between election and predestination? What is the difference between these two terms?
3. How and why is the Spirit the link between the Father's eternal plan of redemption and God's covenant with us in Christ?
4. What does sanctification mean in Scripture? What does Peter mean by the term in this passage?

5. How is holiness or obedience related to our redemption in Christ? Why is this truth so important? How is it related to being sprinkled with Christ's blood?

KNOWING THE FATHER

Chapter Four

The Trinity and How the Father Saves Us

"Blessed be the God and Father of our Lord Jesus Christ, who has blessed us with every spiritual blessing in the heavenly places in Christ, just as He chose us in Him before the foundation of the world, that we should be holy and without blame before Him in love, having predestined us to adoption as sons by Jesus Christ to Himself, according to the good pleasure of His will, to the praise of the glory of His grace, by which He made us accepted in the Beloved." (Ephesians 1:3-6)

In part two of John Bunyan's *Pilgrim's Progress*, Prudence asked Christiana's youngest child three questions: How does the Father save us? How does the Son save us? and How does the Holy Spirit save us? After receiving his answer, Prudence responded, "You are to be commended for thus bringing up your children. I suppose I need not ask the rest these questions, since the youngest of them can answer them so well."[24] Are we accustomed to answering such questions today? The previous chapter gazed at the landscape of the Trinity in the plan of salvation from afar. This chapter and the next two use Ephesians 1:3-14 as Scriptural binoculars to see better the details of the countryside. Verses 3-6 teach us that the Father saves us through blessing us in Christ. This is important because this teaches us how to approach the Father through Christ and how to relate to Him in prayer.

The Father blesses us in Christ alone. This verse highlights a new title for the God of the Old Testament. He is not merely the Almighty, the God who Sees, the God who Provides, and the Great

---

[24] John Bunyan, *The Pilgrim's Progress From this World to That Which is To Come, The Second Part* (London, 1687), 76-77.

I Am. He is the Father of Christ.[25] He is the God and Father of our Lord Jesus Christ before He becomes our God and Father in Christ. "Blessing" is both the theme of verse three and of this entire section (v. 3-14), which is one long sentence in the Greek text. We bless the Father because He has blessed us with every spiritual blessing in the heavenly places in Christ. Peter O'Brien observes that the Father is "the origin and source" of every such blessing.[26] Christ is seated in heaven (Col. 3) and, in Him, the Father incorporates us into the heavenly realm.[27] These blessings are "spiritual" because, whether spiritual or physical, the Holy Spirit is their source (v. 13-14). Eternal life is knowing the Father as the only true God, and Jesus Christ whom He sent (Jn. 17:3). This refers to the quality of life more than the duration of life, since both the godly and the wicked will continue forever, whether in heaven or in hell. Christ is the only Mediator between God and man (1 Tim. 2:5). He is the way, the truth, and the life, and no one comes to the Father except through Him (Jn. 14:6). Do you come to the Father through Him? Bless the Father who blesses us with every spiritual blessing in Christ.

The Father elects and adopts us in Christ (v. 4-5). Election is eternal. The Father chose believers in Christ before they believed and were planted into Christ. As we saw in the previous chapter, He did not choose us because He foresaw that we would chose Him any more than He loved us because He foresaw that we would love Him. We love Him because He first loved us (1 Jn. 4:19) and we choose Him because He first chose us. Christ is God's elect and chosen one in whom His soul delights (Is. 42:1). Christ is "the Chosen One par excellence."[28] The Father chose us in Christ before time began so that, in time, we might resemble Christ by being holy and blameless before Him, and in love He has predestined us to adoption as sons. Both male and female believers are "sons," meaning that they are full heirs. All believers share the status that belonged to the firstborn

---

[25] Peter Thomas O'Brien, *The Letter to the Ephesians* (Grand Rapids, MI: W.B. Eerdmans Publishing Company, 1999), 94.

[26] O'Brien, *Ephesians*, 91.

[27] O'Brien, *Ephesians*, 97.

[28] O'Brien, *Ephesians*, 99.

alone in the ancient world. Adoption summarizes all of the rights and privileges that belong to us in the Gospel by virtue of our personal relation to the Father. Adoption and all of its blessings is the destination to which the Father predestined us according to His purpose of election. We were children of darkness who obeyed the will of our father the devil (Eph. 5:8; Jn. 8:44). In saving us, the Father transferred our family line at the same time that he transferred our citizenship and kingdom (Col. 1:13). Behold what manner of love the Father has bestowed on us, that we should be called the sons of God! (1 Jn. 3:1). He will make us holy and blameless before Him in love at the last day (v. 2). If we have this hope in ourselves, then should we not purify ourselves in holiness even as Christ is pure? (v. 3). Does the Father's electing, predestinating, and adopting love demand anything less?

The Father does all of these things to the praise of His glorious grace. The New Testament elsewhere ascribes grace preeminently to Christ (2 Cor. 13:14). Yet the grace of the Father and of the Spirit is of one piece with the grace of the Son. The Father's grace is refracted through the Son as through a prism. The Father shows the grace of God through blessing us in Christ, according to His purposes of election, by predestinating us to adoption. He demonstrates the grace of God by His plan, even as the Son does through His purchase, and as the Spirit does through applying God's grace to us personally. Is the grace of God glorious to you? Do you praise Him for His glorious grace?

Let us love the Father for loving us with an everlasting love. Let us trust the Father even as we trust Christ, through whom we come to the Father. Let us live as adopted children who long to have blameless lives before the Father, both on earth and in glory.

Study Questions:

1. What new title does the New Testament assign to the God of the Old Testament? Why is this important?
2. What is the nature of eternal life? Why?
3. How does Christ's election by the Father relate to our election by the Father? How does this relate to our adoption by God?
4. How does the grace of the Father relate to the grace of Christ?

KNOWING THE SON

Chapter Five

The Trinity and How the Son Saves Us

"In Him we have redemption through His blood, the forgiveness of sins, according to the riches of His grace which He made to abound toward us in all wisdom and prudence, having made known to us the mystery of His will, according to His good pleasure which He purposed in Himself, that in the dispensation of the fullness of the times He might gather together in one all things in Christ, both which are in heaven and which are on earth—in Him. In Him also we have obtained an inheritance, being predestined according to the purpose of Him who works all things according to the counsel of His will, that we who first trusted in Christ should be to the praise of His glory" (Eph. 1:7–12).

In J.R.R. Tolkien's, *The Hobbit*, Thorin Oakenshield recovers a kingdom full of treasure after the death of the dragon that stole it from him. However, even surrounded by his recovered treasure, Thorin could not be content without one jewel that was worth more to him than an entire mountain full of gold. Jesus Christ is like the crown jewel of the Triune God's work of salvation. Without Him, we could enjoy neither the Father's love nor the Spirit's strengthening hand. He is the jewel that rightly draws the primary attention of our spiritual eyes and through which we treasure the Father's blessings. The previous chapters have shown that the New Testament is Trinitarian in character. However, the Trinitarian theology in the New Testament is a Christ–centered Trinitarianism. As James Durham wrote,

> When the Son is worshipped, there is no less respect to be had to His mediation, than when the Father is expressed; so that whoever be named [Father, Son, or Spirit], the Son still, as Mediator, is to be made use of; for, as there is but One God, so there is but one Mediator

> between God and man. 1 Tim. 2:5. Without whom there is no access for a sinner to approach unto, or worship acceptably, this One God.[29]

No one comes to the Father except through Christ (John 14:6) and the Spirit aims to glorify Him (John 16:11).

This chapter looks at Christ in relation to the Trinity through a telescope. The five subsequent chapters look at Christ in relation to the Trinity through a microscope. These verses teach us that the Father saves us by blessing us in His Son. This means that the Son must be preeminent in our affections and that we must study to know Him.

Christ saves His people from their sins (Eph. 1:7–8; Matt: 1:21). If Christ is the foundation of the Gospel, then knowing God with the forgiveness of our sins is its chief benefit (Heb. 8:12). Sin is a debt that sinners cannot repay, and all have sinned and fallen short of the glory of God (Rom. 3:23). We must be convinced and convicted of sin and turn from our sins to the living God (Acts 3:19). The title, "Christ," appears 15 times in Ephesians 1:3–14.[30] This effectively intertwines Christ's work with the Father and the Spirit, showing the unity of the Trinity in our salvation. "Redemption through His blood" shifts our focus in the passage from election and adoption to redemption and forgiveness of sins as the means of bringing these blessings to fruition. Christ's grace on the cross is rooted in the Father's grace in electing love. We should not attempt to divide the Trinity by saying that the Father chose some men to salvation, that the Son died for all men equally, and that the Spirit calls the elect only to salvation. This would pit the Son against the Father and the Spirit. As Owen noted, Christ died for all men without distinction, but not for all men without exception.[31] Christ gave His life for His sheep (John 10:15) and all whom the Father has given to Him will come to Him (John 6:37). All for whom Christ died also die to sin and will be raised in Christ (2 Cor. 5:14–15).

---

[29] Durham, *A Commentarie upon the Book of the Revelation*, 14.

[30] O'Brien, *Ephesians*, 91.

[31] John Owen, *The Death of Death in the Death of Christ*, in, *The Works of John Owen, D.D.*, ed. William H. Goold, 24 vols. (Edinburgh: Johnstone & Hunter, 1850), 10:173-174, 249, 340.

Christ saves His people by redeeming them. Redemption means that Christ purchased us by paying the price of God's wrath. This means that the cross is the core of the Gospel message (1 Cor. 2:1–5). Our redemption is costly. Christian ministers must preach Christ and His cross if they are to fulfill their commission as Christ's ambassadors (2 Cor. 5:18–21). The cross displays the wisdom and the power of God as much as it reveals "the mystery of His will." Though the cross is foolishness to those who are perishing, it is the wisdom of God for salvation to all who believe (1 Cor. 1:18). Redemption displays the wisdom of God by solving a dilemma that condemned men and baffled angels: How can an infinitely holy God be reconciled to sinners incurring an infinite weight of guilt? God is a just Judge who will by no means clear the guilty (Nah. 1:3). As the God man, Christ represented the offended God and the offending sinner.[32] The love of God to sinners and His wrath against their sins met and shook hands at the cross. He did not clear the guilty, but He took their guilt so that, through faith, they might become the righteousness of God in Him (2 Cor. 5:21). The glorious truth of the Gospel means, "But of Him you are in Christ Jesus, who became for us wisdom from God—and righteousness and sanctification and redemption— that, as it is written, "He who glories, let him glory in the Lord" (1 Cor. 1:30–31). This should set the agenda for our expectations in listening to sermons. While we should look for clear direction to change our practices, is our chief aim to behold the glory of Christ and to know Him better? This alone is what will bring lasting change to our lives, making practical directions in sermons more than moralistic instruction.

Christ saves His people to the uttermost (Eph. 1:9–10; Heb. 7:25). The goal of our redemption is not to look back on a time when we "got saved," but to be part of a new creation in Christ (2 Cor. 5:17; 2 Pet. 3:13). Christ will reconcile all things in heaven and earth (Col. 1:20) by judging the ungodly (Rev. 20:11–15), by resur-

---

[32] See *Westminster Larger Catechism*, question 40: "It was requisite that the Mediator, who was to reconcile God and man, should himself be both God and man, and this in one person, that the proper works of each nature might be accepted of God for us, and relied on by us as the works of the whole person."

recting His people and the world in which they live (Rom. 8:18–24), and by gathering a blessed society of just men made perfect with an innumerable company of angels in heavenly worship (Heb. 12:22–24). Ephesians 1:9–10 are central to the theme of Ephesians and they parallel 3:9–10.[33] O'Brien observes that Christ is the "sphere through whom God sums up the universe."[34] This will culminate in Christ's return. Just as Christ came at the right time (Gal. 4:4), so He will return at the right time. The "mystery" of God's will, which was hidden in election, is revealed to us in Christ now, and will reach its consummation in the age to come. As the Father chose us "in Christ" so He will gather us "in Christ" at the last day.

Christ saves His people for the Father's glory (Eph. 1:11–12). He does so by giving us an inheritance. We are God's inheritance and He is ours (Deut. 32:9; Ps. 16:5). More specifically, the nations redeemed by Christ are His heritage (Ps. 2:8). Both Jews and Gentiles are in view here: "we who first trusted in Christ" and the rest of you (implied). This reconciliation between God and men and between men and each other is described gloriously in Eph. 2:14–18, which culminates in the great Trinitarian statement we have seen above. Redemption in Christ glorifies the Father by bringing us to Him, to the praise of His glory (Eph. 1:12). The Father brings this to pass according to the counsel of His will (Eph. 1:11). He has unconditional freedom and sovereignty to accomplish His purposes. The Father elects according to His will and the Son shares in the counsel of that will and directs all things according to it. Does our conception of the Gospel end with our salvation and with ourselves, or with praising the Father for His glorious grace in Christ?

Cultivate communion with the Son in grace. Do not trust in your own righteousness, but the righteousness that comes through faith in Christ (Phil. 3:9). Flee from worldliness by becoming consumed with Christ, the great treasure of your soul. Look to the new heavens and new earth in which righteousness dwells (2 Peter 3:13) and live as citizens of heaven as you eagerly await the Savior (Phil. 3:20).

---

[33] O'Brien, *Ephesians*, 63.

[34] O'Brien, *Ephesians*, 111.

Study Questions:

1. How and why does the New Testament teach a Christ-centered Trinitarianism? Why do all spiritual blessings come to us from the Father through the Son?
2. How does Christ redeem us?
3. What are the effects of Christ's redemption on believers? What implications does this have for the term "salvation?"
4. What is the goal of salvation? What response does this demand from us?

Chapter Six

The Trinity and Christ's Incarnation

"And the angel answered and said to her, "The Holy Spirit will come upon you, and the power of the Highest will overshadow you; therefore, also, that Holy One who is to be born will be called the Son of God." (Luke 1:35)

Salvation is the work of the triune God. The emphasis of the eternal covenant of redemption falls on Christ's relationship to the Father. The emphasis of the temporal covenant of grace falls on His relationship to the Holy Spirit. The Son of God is not only the second Person in the Trinity. He is Immanuel, God with us (Isa. 7:14). The incarnate Christ is both the second Person of the Trinity acting in human flesh and He is the primary object of the work of the Triune God. In every aspect of Christ's person and work, there is a parallel in the experience of believers. In this chapter we will see that Christ was born of the Spirit so that we might be born of the Spirit.

The incarnate Christ would be the Son of God and the Son of David. In Luke 1:31, the angel Gabriel promised that Mary would conceive and bear a Son and call His name Jesus. He was to be called Jesus because He would save His people from their sins (Matt. 1:21). Like the name Joshua, Jesus means, "Yahweh saves." Verses 32–33 teach that He would be both the Son of the Most High and the Son of David. He was the Son of David according to the flesh, but He was declared to be the Son of God with power by His resurrection from the dead (Rom. 1:4). This Person had two parentages: one divine and one human. He would be fully God and fully man, in two distinct natures and one person forever.[35] As the God-man, He would become the King of an everlasting kingdom (Luke 1:33;

[35] *Westminster Shorter Catechism*, question 21.

Dan. 7:27). Mary responded to the angel by asking how these things could be (Luke 1:34). This was not a question of doubt as Zechariah's earlier question was (v. 18); rather, she was asking what she should do. Mary believed in the fact of Christ's incarnation better than she understood it. Is it so with you? You must believe what the Scriptures teach about the identity of Christ as true God and true man.

The incarnation was a work of the entire Trinity. Mary would conceive the Child when the Holy Spirit came upon her (Luke 1:35). This would come to pass through the power of the Most High. The Most High here refers to the Father, since it does so clearly in v. 32 where Christ is called His Son. The Father exercised His power in the incarnation through the work of the Holy Spirit in conceiving the Christ. Yet it was the Son whose person was united to human nature in this act. Neither the Father nor the Spirit took on human flesh. Here we see again that the three divine Persons work simultaneously in every divine act, yet they act according to their particular personal properties. The Son was incarnated by the Father's power through the operation of the Holy Spirit. The undivided works of the Godhead always reflect the work appropriate to each divine Person. The unity of the Godhead requires that no divine Person can be excluded from any act of God. The distinction of the Persons means that each divine Person highlights a distinct facet of God's work. This is like admiring a multi-sided jewel. The wonder of the incarnation is that Jesus was now the Son of God by His extraordinary birth as well as by His eternal relation to the Father. This is not a sentimental story about a baby born in a manger, but it is about the Lord of Glory coming to earth and becoming man. Do you believe in the incarnation as an act of the triune God?

The incarnation is vital for our salvation. It was vital for Christ to complete His work. We cannot separate Christ's work from His person. Just as the first Adam sinned and ruined the human race, so we needed a second Adam, who through His righteous act could make many righteous (Rom. 5:18–19). Christ needed to take on the nature of His people (Heb. 2:16). He was born of a woman so that He might obey the law and suffer death for us and so that we might be adopted as God's children (Gal. 4:4).[36] However, Christ's divine nature gave infinite dignity to His person. His dignity was commensurate to the eternal debt that we owed to God.[37] He who received the Spirit had the power to give the Spirit. As the God-man, He possesses both divine and human righteousness. He is the only mediator between God and man (1 Tim. 2:5) because He is the only one who is both God and man. Christ satisfies the demands of God and the needs of man by means of His person and work. Just as Christ was conceived by the power of the Holy Spirit, so you must be born of the Spirit if you would see the kingdom of God (John 3:4–5). Christ's supernatural birth must be the grounds of your supernatural birth.

Do you have a new nature? Have you been born of the Spirit? Do you have new life in you through the Spirit, so that you might live in Christ and through Christ to the Father? Do you know these things by exercising faith in Jesus Christ and repentance unto life?

Study Questions:

1. Why is it important to draw parallels between Christ's life and ours? What is the parallel between Christ's incarnation and the Spirit's work in believers?
2. How did each divine Person work in Christ's incarnation?
3. Why is Christ's incarnation vital for our salvation?

---

[36] *Westminster Larger Catechism*, question 39 asserts, "It was requisite that the Mediator should be man, that he might advance our nature, perform obedience to the law, suffer and make intercession for us in our nature, have a fellow-feeling of our infirmities; that we might receive the adoption of sons, and have comfort and access with boldness unto the throne of grace."

[37] *Westminster Larger Catechism*, question 38 states, "It was requisite that the Mediator should be God, that he might sustain and keep the human nature from sinking under the infinite wrath of God, and the power of death, give worth and efficacy to his sufferings, obedience, and intercession; and to satisfy God's justice, procure his favour, purchase a peculiar people, give his Spirit to them, conquer all their enemies, and bring them to everlasting salvation."

Chapter Seven

The Trinity and Christ's Life and Ministry

"Then Jesus came from Galilee to John at the Jordan to be baptized by him. And John tried to prevent Him, saying, "I need to be baptized by You, and are You coming to me?" But Jesus answered and said to him, 'Permit it to be so now, for thus it is fitting for us to fulfill all righteousness.' Then he allowed Him. When He had been baptized, Jesus came up immediately from the water; and behold, the heavens were opened to Him, and He saw the Spirit of God descending like a dove and alighting upon Him. And suddenly a voice came from heaven, saying, 'This is My beloved Son, in whom I am well pleased.'" (Matt. 3:13–17)

Christ was anointed "with the Holy Spirit and power" (Acts 10:38). He was anointed with the Spirit in three stages. The first was at His birth, the second was at His baptism, and the third was upon His ascension. The title, "Christ," means anointed one. In His birth, He was qualified to fulfill His offices of prophet, priest, and king. His baptism marked his public calling to fulfill His public ministry. At His ascension, He poured forth His Spirit on the Church to spread the Gospel and to apply the benefits of redemption on an unprecedented scale (Acts 2:33). Christ's birth by the Spirit inaugurated a life of dependent communion with God. The Spirit's presence at Christ's baptism commenced a public ministry lived out of communion with God. Christ's life in communion with God is the ground and pattern of the Christian's life in communion with God.

Christ's baptism marked the beginning of His public ministry. John was surprised that Christ wanted to be baptized by him. He confessed that he needed Christ to baptize him and not vice versa. This is an implicit confession of Christ's sinlessness. Jesus told John to permit His baptism in order to "fulfill all righteousness." Though

John's baptism was commanded in the Old Testament, yet Jesus received baptism to signify His identification with penitent sinners, such as those whom John was baptizing. Just as all three divine Persons were present and active in His birth, so they were at His baptism. The Son was baptized. The Holy Spirit descended upon Him as a dove. The Father spoke from heaven declaring His great pleasure in His beloved Son. The Father, who sent the Son to fulfill His eternal plan of redemption, now declared openly His approval of the Son in His work. Just as Christ always depended on the Holy Spirit to live a righteous life, so now He would depend on the Spirit in the public exercises of His threefold office. The Spirit was the means by which Christ would finish the work that the Father gave Him to do (John 4:34; 17:4).

Christ's baptism set the tone for His public ministry. This was a ministry of Word and Spirit. He exercised this ministry as a Prophet, as a Priest, and as a King. Just as all three Persons of the Godhead were present at His baptism, so they were active throughout His earthly ministry. The Spirit drove Him into the wilderness to be tempted by Satan (Mark 1:12). He performed miracles and cast out devils by the Spirit of God (Matt. 12:28). He did so as well at the will and command of His Father (John 5:19). He did not do His miraculous works merely by showing a flash of His own divine power. He did so at the command of the Father and by the power of the Holy Spirit. The content of His preaching was from the Father (John 8:38) and He preached as one filled with the Spirit (Luke 4:15). At His transfiguration, the Father once again proclaimed His pleasure in His beloved Son and urged the disciples to listen to Him (Mark 9:7). It was as though the Father pointed to His baptism as the decisive reminder of who His Son was and what He came to do as the God-man. Christ ministered the Word of the Father in the power of the Spirit. In the same way, He continues to speak and to minister to His Church by His Word and Spirit. Do you have a high esteem for the Word of God? Do you believe whatever Christ tells you and are you willing to do whatever He commands you? Do you pray for the Spirit of God to bless you as you read and hear the Bible? No one can confess that Jesus is Lord except though the Spirit of God (1 Cor. 12:3). No one can know the mind of God except through the Spirit of God (1 Cor. 2:11). Receive the Father's Word in humble dependence on the Spirit of Christ. This requires fervent prayer and sincere faith.

Christ's baptism and earthly ministry qualified Him to fulfill His office as Mediator. As our prophet, He revealed the Father to us (John 1:18). As our priest, He fulfilled all righteousness by living a holy life and by dying an accursed death (Heb. 9–10). He fulfilled the requirements of the law and He bore the penalties of the law (Gal. 3:13; 4:1–4). As our king, He received the gifts and graces of the Spirit without measure (Jn. 3:34) so that He might distribute them by measure through Spirit to His Church (Eph. 4:7, 1 Cor. 12:7–11). His baptism shows us that the Church must look to Christ for every blessing from God's hand. We always receive the benefits of redemption indirectly and not directly. Even Christ's promises are means of laying hold of His person and, in Him, all the benefits of redemption. Christ here gives us a pattern for service. He used the gifts of the Spirit from the Father for the good of the Church. Do you use your spiritual gifts for the good of the Church? Do you complain that your gifts are underappreciated when your local church does not let you sing a solo? Or are you willing to deny your sense of self-importance in order to serve the Church in any way that you can? The Son of Man came not to be served but to serve and to give His life as a ransom for many (Mark 10:45). Trust in Christ both as the foundation for your justification and the pattern for your sanctification. Do so by cultivating the graces of the Spirit as you use the gifts of the Spirit.

Christ's life in communion with God is the pattern for your life in communion with God.

Study Questions:

1. Why was Christ baptized if He had no need for repentance and for the forgiveness of sins?
2. How does Christ's baptism relate to His threefold office of Prophet, Priest, and King?
3. How did Christ's baptism and His earthly ministry qualify Him to exercise His office as Mediator?

Chapter Eight

The Trinity and Christ's Death

"For if the blood of bulls and goats and the ashes of a heifer, sprinkling the unclean, sanctifies for the purifying of the flesh, how much more shall the blood of Christ, who through the eternal Spirit offered Himself without spot to God, cleanse your conscience from dead works to serve the living God?" (Heb. 9:13–14)

Christ brings us to the Father through the Spirit. He does so through His death as much as by His life, if not more so. Paul used preaching the cross as shorthand for preaching Christ and His Gospel (1 Cor. 2:1–5). Christ is taking us somewhere. He is taking us from death, sin and hell, to His Father. The road on which He takes us to the Father is through His blood, which He offered to God by the Holy Spirit. We often think of the cross as the action of Christ for His people. It is that and more. Christ's death was an act of the entire Trinity.

Sin requires death (Rom. 6:23; Gen. 2:17). Sin is the black backdrop on which the Gospel is set. The blood of the Old Testament sacrifices preached this truth eloquently. Either we must die for sin in body and soul, or Christ must offer Himself, soul and body, as a sacrifice for our sins (Isa. 53:10). Much like the New Testament sacraments of Baptism and the Lord's Supper, believers in the Old Testament received Christ by faith through the sacrifices. The blood of bulls and goats could not atone for sin (Heb. 10:4). David represented the faith of all believers when he acknowledged this fact (Ps. 40:6; 51:16; Heb. 10:8). He taught that true blessing comes through the remission of sins in Christ alone (Rom. 4:7–10). The cross was a great transaction in which Christ, who knew no sin, became sin for us, that we might become the righteousness of God in Him (2 Cor. 5:21). This is the righteousness that comes through faith (Rom. 3:22). The blood of bulls and goats "sanctified" sinners for the purification of their flesh (Heb. 9:13). This act directed them to what Christ would do for them. This is the background of Hebrews 9-10. We must have this righteousness that comes through faith in Christ and not by the works of the law (Rom. 3:28). Do you rest in the work of Christ on the cross and not in works of righteousness that you have done? (Titus 3:5). The just must live by His faith (Hab. 2:4).

Christ's death was His own act. He offered Himself freely and voluntarily. He was a lamb without spot and without blemish (1 Pet. 1:19). Some abuse the Lord's Supper by treating it as a continual sacrifice of Christ. Those who do so transform the cross into the nature of the Old Testament sacrifices, which could never take away sins. What appears at first glance to be a high view of the Lord's Supper is actually a low view of the finality and sufficiency of Christ's death. Christ offered himself once and for all to "purify our conscience from dead works to serve the living God" (Heb. 9:14). Come to the Lord's Supper as David came to the sacrifices, in order to lay hold of Christ by faith. Faith is the empty beggar's hand that receives Christ. You must come to God through Christ's acts of grace and not through your own works (Rom. 11:6).

Christ accomplished His death through the Spirit (Heb. 9:14). Just as He was baptized with the Spirit, performed miracles by the Spirit, and was led by the Spirit, so the Spirit led Him as a lamb to the slaughter on the cross. He offered Himself to God by the eternal Spirit. As Christ was led by the Spirit, even so as many as are led by the Spirit are the sons of God (Rom. 8:14). The Spirit leads us to Christ whom He led to the cross, and through Him He leads us to God. This is why we must take up the cross and die daily in order to follow Christ (Luke 9:23). We must be led by the Spirit in a life of holiness in conformity to Christ's holiness (Rom. 6:5–11). We must be led by the Spirit to suffer for righteousness sake (Matt. 5:14–16) even as Christ suffered for us and gave Himself once for us, the just for the unjust (1 Peter 3:18). Trust in the Spirit to follow the lamb wherever He goes (Rev. 14:4). Even if He calls you to deny yourself by suffering hardship through obeying Him in every area of life.[38]

[38] For the principle and practical examples of self-denial, see Ryan M. McGraw, *Why Should I Deny Myself?, Cultivating Biblical Godliness* (Grand Rapids, MI: Reformation Heritage Books, 2015).

Christ offered His sacrificial death to God the Father. The Father here represents the violated honor of the entire Trinity. This raises two questions. First, to whom did Christ offer Himself? It is popular to say that He paid the price to Satan. Yet Satan is merely the jailor of the offended Judge. Christ's death broke the power of this jailor over believers (Heb. 2:14), but He paid the price to the Judge and not to the jailor. He offered Himself to God. Second, who crucified Christ? Was it the Jews? Was it the Romans? Was it Satan, who filled Judas's heart with the evil plan to betray Him? (Luke 22:3; John13:27). It was all of these, yet in different ways. Both Jews and Gentiles took Him and killed Him by lawless hands (Acts 2:23). Satan assaulted Him with all the malice he was capable of. Yet this happened by the predetermined counsel and foreknowledge of God (Acts 2:23). The cross was simultaneously the greatest act of human and demonic wickedness and the clearest proof of the Father's love (1 John 4:9). Do not give Satan more credit than he deserves by putting the cross in his hands. Christ paid a ransom to His Father when He offered Himself to God by the eternal Spirit. Through the "eternal Spirit," the Father gives "eternal redemption" to those who trust in Christ's blood.

As Christ offered Himself to the Father through the Spirit, so you must come by the Spirit, through Christ, to the Father.

Study Questions:

1. How does the problem of sin relate to the good news of the Gospel? How should you respond to the knowledge of your sin?
2. How were the Father and the Spirit at work in Christ's death?
3. To whom did Christ offer Himself on the cross? Why is the answer to this question important?

Chapter Nine
The Trinity and Christ's Resurrection

"But you are not in the flesh but in the Spirit, if indeed the Spirit of God dwells in you. Now if anyone does not have the Spirit of Christ, he is not His. And if Christ is in you, the body is dead because of sin, but the Spirit is life because of righteousness. But if the Spirit of Him who raised Jesus from the dead dwells in you, He who raised Christ from the dead will also give life to your mortal bodies through His Spirit who dwells in you." (Rom. 8:9–11)

Most of us appreciate the sun.[39] We enjoy its warmth as the flowers bloom in spring and turn their faces toward it as to a faithful and life-giving benefactor. Yet the sun often serves as a backdrop to our day while we often do not actively meditate on how necessary it is to sustain our lives and how greatly it proclaims to us God's glory (Ps. 19:4–6). One of my fellow elders in Sunnyvale is a solar physicist. He spends a great deal of his time studying the glory of the sun and, as a faithful believer in Christ, he strives to do so to the glory of his Creator. He sees wonders in this part of God's creation that few realize, even though all enjoy its benefits. So it is with the doctrine of the Trinity for most Christians. God's Triunity ties together all of the strands of the Gospel in the person and work of Jesus Christ, including His resurrection. The Trinity is the tapestry into which the doctrines of the New Testament are woven and without which our salvation would disappear. However, just as we rarely contemplate the glory of the sun in creation, many believers underappreciate the Trinitarian backdrop of their redemption. We need to bring the Trinity, which often stands in the background of

---

[39] This chapter appeared as an article by Ryan M. McGraw, *"The Trinity and Christ's Resurrection," New Horizons*, April 2015, 3–5. Used with permission.

our faith and life as Christians, into the foreground of our Christian experience and worship.

Developing a self-conscious trinitarian devotion can help us greatly in contemplating the glorious significance of Christ's resurrection. The passage cited above teaches us the following precious truths about the work of the entire Trinity in connection to Christ's resurrection and in our lives as believers: By His resurrection, Christ lives to His Father by the power of the Spirit. Through His resurrection, believers also live to the Father by the power of the Spirit. This sets the pattern for Christian life and experience, both in this life and in the life to come. Believers live to God by the Spirit because Christ lives to God by the Spirit. They do so in their personal holiness in this life, and in the resurrection of the body in the next life. Our relation to each divine Person in verses 9-11 corresponds to the blessings described in verses 12–17, giving us a full picture of how the Triune God works both in Christ's resurrection and in ours. The following meditations are designed to stir up your faith, love, and hope in the Father, who raised His Son from the dead on your behalf, by the power of the Holy Spirit.

The Spirit of God and of Christ dwells in believers by virtue of Christ's resurrection (v. 9–11a). The apostle Paul presents this as the fundamental reason why we must serve and obey God. While gratitude is the primary motive for our personal holiness, the indwelling of the Spirit of Christ makes our personal holiness possible. If we are believers, then we have been crucified with Christ and we have been raised in Christ to walk in newness of life (Gal. 2:20; Rom. 6:4; Col. 3:1). This is a past action in relation to Christ's resurrection rather than a prediction of a future bodily resurrection. As a result of union with Christ in His resurrection, Paul says that believers are no longer "in the flesh." This means that they are no longer driven solely by the impulses of their sinful nature. For this reason, he exhorts us elsewhere, "Neither yield ye your members as instruments of unrighteousness unto sin: but yield yourselves unto God, as those that are alive from the dead, and your members as instruments of righteousness unto God" (Rom. 6:13). Believers live in the Spirit of God and the Spirit of God lives in them. There is a mutual interpenetration between believers and the Spirit that mimics, in a dim way, the interpenetration of the Persons of the Godhead. Christ applied this teaching to our relation to the Father and to the Son as well in John 14–17 (John 14:20, 23; 17:23). The Spirit is the Spirit of God and the Spirit of Christ. The Father sent the Spirit to dwell in believers through His Son, who purchased the gift of the Spirit for them. In His indwelling presence, the Spirit of God is the life of God manifested in the regenerate soul. This is why Paul says that if we do not have the Spirit of God then we are "none of His." These truths correspond to the Spirit's work in mortifying sin in Rom. 8:13–14. When Christ rose from the dead, He was "justified in the Spirit" (1 Tim. 3:16). The Spirit who declared Him righteous now declares believers righteous in Christ because they are united to Christ by faith (Phil. 3:9). But the Father does not only declare us righteous in Christ. The Spirit makes us righteous in practice by conforming us to the image of Christ. Does the Spirit of God who dwelt in Christ dwell in you? Is He directing your life to the Father in obedience to Christ? Obedience is the true mark of the Spirit-filled life.

Christ dwells in believers and manifests His resurrected life in them (v. 10). He enables the Spirit of life to dwell in them. The indwelling Spirit makes it possible to love and obey God because He unites us to Christ, who is our life (Col. 3:4). We draw spiritual vitality from Christ as branches draw life and bear fruit from the vine (John 15:1ff). The Christian's life in Christ entails death as well as life. If you are alive in Christ, then "the body is dead because of sin." Previously you were dead to God and alive to sin (Rom. 7:9, implied). Now in Christ, you are dead to sin and alive to God (Rom. 6:11). You carry the remnants of sin with you and they taint everything you do. This is why question 82 of the *Shorter Catechism* asserts, "No mere man, since the fall, is able, in this life, perfectly to keep the commandments of God; but doth daily break them, in thought, word, and deed." However, the "old man" in you is both dead and dying (Rom. 6:6; 4:22). This is why question 35 in the catechism also asserts, "Sanctification is the work of God's free grace, whereby we are renewed in the whole man after the image of God, and are enabled more and more to die unto sin, and live unto righteousness." The old man died when you were united to Christ and when you were relieved from all condemnation. Yet sin remains and we must put to death and put off the old man and his sinful deeds (Col. 3:5). The indwelling of Christ corresponds to our being joint heirs with Christ in verse 17. Because the resurrected Christ dwells within believers, they are identified with Him in His exaltation and they partake of His inheritance. This is why Paul refers to our own resurrection in Christ and the accompanying transformation of our world as eagerly awaiting our adoption (Rom. 8:23). Does the risen Christ dwell in you? Is the life of the Spirit manifested in you by producing righteousness in you? Do you show this by hating sin for Christ's sake? The life of Christ in us should lead us to hate the nature of sin as against God more than we hate the consequences of sin against ourselves. Does the life that is in you through the power of God long and strive for conformity to the resurrected Christ, who is both the source and pattern of that life? The mortification of sin and obedience to God's law are the primary ways that you must manifest the life and presence of the glorified Christ in you.

The Father grants life to believers on the ground of Christ's resurrection (v. 11). This verse explicitly mentions all three Persons of the Godhead. While the Father's personal name does not appear in the text, Paul refers to the Holy Spirit as "the Spirit of him that raised up Jesus from the dead." Paul indicates that the Father raised Christ from the dead. Similarly, Jesus indicates elsewhere that it is the Father who sends the indwelling Spirit to believers in Christ's name (John 14:26). He sends the Spirit to believers in Christ's name because the Spirit's work in believers is secured by and grounded on the finished work of Christ. It is in light of such truths that Paul argues that He who raised Christ from the dead by the Spirit will raise Christ's people from the dead by the Spirit as well. The same Spirit who breathes spiritual life into our souls at the new birth will breathe physical life into our "mortal bodies" at the resurrection. We benefit from Christ's resurrection right now through living godly lives. The resurrection of our bodies at the last day will be the final consummation of the benefits we receive from being united from Christ in his resurrection. Life in Christ now will give way to a perfected life in body and soul in glory. If verses 9–10 demonstrate the power of the Spirit of Christ, who enables us to live holy lives, then verse 11 provides us with a motive to live in light of His powerful work in us. This is where gratitude must come into holy living and where verses 9-11 receive their complement in verses 12–17, which read,

> Therefore, brethren, we are debtors—not to the flesh, to live according to the flesh. For if you live according to the flesh you will die; but if by the Spirit you put to death the deeds of the body, you will live. For as many as are led by the Spirit of God, these are sons of God. For you did not receive the spirit of bondage again to fear, but you received the Spirit of adoption by whom we cry out, "Abba, Father." The Spirit Himself bears witness with our spirit that we are children of God, and if children, then heirs—heirs of God and joint heirs with Christ, if indeed we suffer with Him, that we may also be glorified together.

The Spirit of Him who raised Christ Jesus from the dead (v. 11) corresponds in this passage to the Spirit of adoption dwelling in our hearts, through whom we cry, "Abba, Father" (v. 15–16). The Spirit of adoption with whom we have communion in this life will culminate in the full experience and revelation of our adoption in a perfected and resurrected world (v. 21–23). Do you not have the highest motives to persevere in a godly life? Does this not furnish you with more than adequate grounds to be assured that if the Spirit of Christ is in you, and if Christ Himself is in you, and if the Father will resurrect you, that you can persevere by faith and obedience in fellowship with God? Truly, "Who shall separate us from the love of Christ?" (v. 35). Let us persevere joyfully in faith and obedience to Christ, for "He that raised up Christ from the dead shall also quicken your mortal bodies by His Spirit that dwelleth in you" (v. 11).

Not all ministers and churches celebrate the holiday known as Easter (myself included among them, in case you are wondering). Leaving off the question of observing special days for worship not mandated in Scripture, Paul's teaching on the Trinity in relation to Christ's resurrection and to the believer highlights the fact that we should not need a holiday to live in light of the resurrection. The power of the triune God in relation to Christ's resurrection and as applied to us by the Spirit touches every day and every moment of the Christian life, from the new birth to the Day of Judgment. We ought to celebrate the resurrection every Lord's Day, but this should be only the beginning. Even when we remember the Sabbath day, we do so, "partly, because of the great benefit of remembering it, we being thereby helped in our preparation to keep it, and, in keeping it, better to keep all the rest of the commandments, and to continue a thankful remembrance of the two great benefits of creation and redemption, which contain a short abridgment of religion" (Q&A 121). Our celebration of the Trinity and Christ's resurrection on the Lord's Day should spill over into living godly lives through faith in Christ's resurrection and looking in hope to the perfect and final sanctification of our souls and bodies at the last day. Just as my friend and fellow elder can better appreciate the benefits of living under the sun because he is a solar physicist, so we as Christians ought better to appreciate and to love Christ's resurrection as we dwell in communion with the Father, through His Son, by His Spirit.

Live a holy life to God, by the Spirit, in union with Christ. This is the fruit of Christ's resurrection and the product of communion with the entire Trinity.

Study Questions:

1. How does the doctrine of the Trinity help us understand better Christ's resurrection? How did all three Persons work in His resurrection?
2. How does Christ's resurrection relate to the indwelling of the Spirit in believers? How is this related to our sanctification and our pursuit of personal holiness?
3. How is our sanctification related to our union with Christ?
4. How and why is Christ's resurrection connected to our own?
5. How can we use the Lord's Day to remember Christ's resurrection? How should doing so affect our Christian living?

Chapter Ten

The Trinity and Christ's Ascension

"Therefore being exalted to the right hand of God, and having received from the Father the promise of the Holy Spirit, He poured out this which you now see and hear." (Acts 2:33)

Christ received the Spirit from the Father in order to expand and to govern the Church. Christ always possessed the Spirit without measure (John 3:34), but on His ascension, He received the Spirit for a new purpose. He received the Spirit in order to pour Him out upon others. In this verse, Peter appeals to this fact in order to explain the outpouring of the Spirit's gifts on the Church. Though the Spirit gives gifts to men, He is also the primary gift of Christ to His people. He both leads people into communion with God and He equips the Church in its mission to lead others into communion with God. The primary mission of the Spirit is to spread the Gospel of Christ and to bring men and women to the Father. This is Christ's third anointing with the Spirit. Christ received the Spirit from the Father in order to equip the Church to testify to Christ. This is the primary ground of hope as we bear witness to Christ before the world.

Christ received the Spirit by His exaltation to the Father's right hand. This is why John wrote earlier that the Spirit had not yet been given since Jesus had not yet been glorified (John 7:37). Though the Spirit hovered over the face of the deep in the creation (Gen. 1:2), led Israel through the wilderness (Ex. 13:21), spoke by the prophets (1 Peter 1:11), and taught the necessity of the new birth even in the Old Testament (John 3:10), He was now working in a new way. His work following Christ's ascension would be so great that nothing He had done prior to this event could compare to it. This work is attached to and results from Christ's ascension. We will see in a subsequent chapter that Christ's ascension marked His mediatorial reign over the Church in which He sovereignly gives gifts to men (Eph. 4:11ff). Christ's ascension introduced the era of the Holy Spirit. The importance of the ascension goes far beyond the gifts that Christ gave. Our ascended King reigns in heaven over the Church and in the world by His Spirit. Do you rightly value Christ's ascension?

Christ received the Spirit by the Father's gift. This shows the voluntary condescension of the Spirit. Though He is God equal with the Father and with the Son, He proceeded from the Father through the Son to the Church (John 15:26). All three divine Persons are united in every work of God. The Spirit has one will with the Father and the Son and fulfills His work in the plan of redemption conducting the harmonious symphony of the Godhead. As the Spirit proceeds from the Father and the Son from all eternity, so the Spirit works from the Father through the Son in history. Christ did not receive the Spirit as gift for His own sake, but for our sakes. The Father promises to give the Holy Spirit to those who ask Him (Luke 11:13). He does so through the Son and in response to prayer in the Son's name (John 14:12–14). This order of divine operation means that the Spirit is a Christ-centered Spirit. He proceeds from Christ, and He leads men and women to Christ (John 15:23; 16:8–11). By bringing people to Christ, He brings them to the Father in whom they have life and an eternal inheritance. This is what He was doing in Acts 2 on the day of Pentecost. This is what He continues to do today when men, like Peter, preach the Word of God. This means that glorifying Christ should be the aim of every preacher and of every sermon, if they desire the Spirit to second their preaching in people's hearts. Do you pray that the Spirit would glorify Christ in your heart as you read the Bible and hear it preached? Do you know that Christ has received the Spirit through experiencing the Spirit's power from Christ and through Christ?

Christ poured out the Spirit whom He received from the Father. Peter says that His works were both seen and heard. The disciples saw them when He came upon them in tongues of fire (Acts 2:3). The crowds saw them through apostolic miracles (Heb. 2:4). Both heard them when the disciples spoke of the "mighty works of

God" so that everyone understood them in his own language (Acts 2:4–6, 11). The emphasis in the narrative in Acts is on the Spirit's power in converting sinners through the preaching of the Gospel. He demonstrated His power when the crowd was "cut to the heart" and cried out, "Brothers, what shall we do?" (Acts 2:37). We should marvel at the evidences of His continuing work today when we see so many who profess Christ's name from every tribe, tongue, people, and nation. This work began in Acts and it continues at present. It is Christ's work, from the Father, by the Spirit, in fulfilling the mission of the Church. Do you look to Christ to pour out the Spirit today? Do you come with expectation to the preaching of the Word? Does His Word affect you powerfully? You must receive Christ by faith through the Spirit's work if you would come to the Father.

Trust in Christ to equip the Church to bring men to the Father through the Spirit.

Study Questions:

1. How is Christ's ascension related to the outpouring of the Holy Spirit? How does this relate to the spread of the Gospel?
2. How does the Spirit work differently in the Old and New Testaments? Why is this important to the Church today?
3. How is the Spirit's work resulting from Christ's ascension related to preaching?
4. How do we see evidences of the Spirit's work in the world today? How should this encourage us in our evangelism?

KNOWING THE SPIRIT

Chapter Eleven

The Trinity and How the Spirit Saves Us

"In Him you also trusted, after you heard the word of truth, the gospel of your salvation; in whom also, having believed, you were sealed with the Holy Spirit of promise, who is the guarantee of our inheritance until the redemption of the purchased possession, to the praise of His glory" (Eph. 1:13–14).

The Father's election and the Son's redemption would be like Ezekiel's reassembled and lifeless bones unless the Holy Spirit breathed life into them (Ezek. 37:1–14). The problem is not with God, but with people who are dead in trespasses and sins (Eph. 2:1). The Spirit is the breath of life to the Christian soul. Unless we are born of water and of the Spirit, we cannot enter the kingdom of God (Jn. 3:5). The Spirit was Christ's constant companion (John 3:34; etc.) and He should be ours as well. The Spirit "stamps His character" on every blessing and guarantees their fulfillment.[40] The Spirit saves us as the seal and the down payment of our inheritance in Christ.

The Spirit saves us by enabling us to receive Christ. This has often been called "effectual calling," since not everyone who hears the call of the Gospel receives the Spirit's call in their hearts. *Westminster Shorter Catechism*, question thirty one, teaches us, "Effectual calling is the work of God's Spirit, whereby, convincing us of our sin and misery, enlightening our minds in the knowledge of Christ, and renewing our wills, He doth persuade and enable us to embrace Jesus Christ, freely offered to us in the Gospel." As the Spirit opened Lydia's heart to receive Christ (Acts 16:14), so He does with all who are appointed to eternal life (Acts 13:48). This is a perfect mirror of the Father's plan and the Son's purchase. Those who sin are slaves to

---

[40] O'Brien, *Ephesians*, 92.

sin (Jn. 8:34). We were willing and ignorant slaves, obeying the will of our father the devil and wanting to do it, without knowing that he was our father (John 8:44). The Spirit frees us from sin and makes us willing slaves to righteousness (Rom. 6:18). As the teacher of our hearts, the Spirit enables us to be taught of God (John 6:45). This reveals the fact that the Father and Christ call sinners, but not in the same way as the Spirit. Their work does not add up to three parts of an action, but they represent three facets of the same work. The Father calls sinners to Christ by His Word and Spirit.

The Spirit saves us as the seal of our redemption in Christ. The Spirit is mentioned in our text in relation to His work after we believe the Gospel rather than our calling to receive Christ in the Gospel. Yet the Spirit's work in enabling us to believe the Gospel is related to His work in sealing us for salvation. You may have heard the term "seal" in relation to Baptism and the Lord's Supper. Analogously to these ordinances, Paul wrote that Abraham's circumcision was a seal to him of the righteousness that he received by faith (Rom. 4:11). A seal is a stamp of ownership or authenticity, much like a king's signet ring that he used to mark royal documents. We must understand the sacrament as seals in light of the Holy Spirit's work as the seal of our redemption. Note that we are "sealed with the Holy Spirit." Sealing is not so much something that the Spirit does to believers as it is something that He is in relation to believers. The "sealing" of the Spirit is virtually equal to the indwelling of the Spirit that commences with our regeneration. They were sealed with the Spirit simultaneously to their believing. The Father set His seal upon Christ (John 6:27) by the miracles that He performed by the Spirit. The Spirit is the Spirit "of promise" because He is the content of the promise. Every "good thing" we seek from God in prayer is summarized in the gift of the Holy Spirit Himself (Matt. 7:11 with Luke 11:13). Every divine blessing communicated to us comes through the Spirit and the goal of all of the Spirit's blessings to us aims at communion with God. This means that we should pray even for physical needs with spiritual aims. The sealing of the Spirit should not be equated with personal assurance of salvation, though it is the ground of such assurance. As we grieve the Spirit, who sealed us for the day of redemption, through ungodly living (Eph. 4:30–31), so we express the Spirit's sealing work by being "kind to one another, tenderhearted, forgiving one another, even as God in Christ forgave you" (Eph. 4:32). Foster communion with the Spirit by walking with God in heart, speech, and behavior. He is the document of the King that assures us of our certificate in Christ by which we enter into the King's court.

The Spirit saves us as the down payment of our inheritance. We often speak wrongly about owning our homes. Most of us have made down payments only, which are pledges of future installments leading to future ownership. Paul only uses this terminology in the New Testament and he always uses it of the Holy Spirit.[41] The spirit is a down payment or, "guarantee," of our purchased inheritance in Christ. In the Spirit, we have a partial possession of heaven while we are on earth. The earnest of the Spirit is a pledge that we shall possess the whole. Unlike home ownership, Christ has already paid our debts and we have the title to our inheritance through the Father's adoption. We have the right and the title to the kingdom, but we have only partial possession while we remain on earth. Our communion with the Holy Spirit on earth is a piece of heaven. Should we not use every means to cultivate fellowship with the Spirit now? A Spirit-filled life is part of our present enjoyment of glory. This does not involve the Spirit "telling" us what to eat for breakfast or which person to marry. It entails the Spirit applying Christ to us continually through His Word. Pray fervently for the Spirit's blessings. Pray ultimately for the Spirit Himself to be with us and to work in us. We should pray particularly for His presence in our public worship. Without him, we may as well write "Ichabod" over our sermons and our worship services. Through Him, public worship on earth should become a foretaste of heavenly worship.

Cultivate communion with the Holy Spirit through godly living, by meditation on His work as seal and guarantee, and by fervent prayer that He would glorify Christ in us and through us.

---

[41] O'Brien, *Ephesians*, 121.

Study Questions:

1. Why is the Spirit's work necessary for our salvation?
2. What does it mean that the Spirit is the seal of our redemption?
3. How is the Spirit the earnest of our inheritance in Christ? What implications does this have for the Christian life?
4. How does the Spirit's work relate to our prayer lives?

Chapter Twelve
The Trinity and Adoption

"But when the fullness of the time had come, God sent forth His Son, born of a woman, born under the law, to redeem those who were under the law, that we might receive the adoption as sons. And because you are sons, God has sent forth the Spirit of His Son into your hearts, crying out, "Abba, Father!"" (Gal. 4:4–6)

Adoption summarizes all of the rights and privileges that belong to us as God's children.[42] When Christians adopt children, they bring those who were "strangers to the covenants of promise" (Eph. 2:12), into the Church, which is the kingdom of God's dear Son (Col. 1:13). However, the Church should pray joyfully that a more important adoption would take place among all of its children. We pray that our children would be more God's children than our own children. Every true Christian is a firstborn child and heir of the King of Kings and Lord of Lords. Out text teaches us that the Father sent His Son in order to give us the Spirit of adoption.[43] Though this is properly an act of the Father, it appears in this section under the Spirit since the Spirit brings us to experience the glories of our adoption by God.

God sent His Son at the right time, in the right way, and for the right purpose (v. 4). Christ came at the right time. "The fullness of the time" was the time that God appointed to send His Son to save sinners. The God of both Jews and Gentiles chose to send His Son to justify sinners through faith without the works of the law (Rom.

[42] *Westminster Shorter Catechism*, question 34: "Adoption is an act of God's free grace, whereby we are received into the number, and have a right to all the privileges of, the sons of God."

[43] Adoption is really a work appropriate to the Father. However, I have included adoption under the Spirit's work in salvation because the Spirit brings our adoption to fruition through Christ, bringing us into God's family.

3:28–29). Christ came in the right way. He had to be made like us in every way, yet without sin, in order to qualify Him to help us (Heb. 4:14–16). He was "made of a woman." He did not take the nature of angels, but He took the nature of Abraham's children (Heb. 2:16). "Know ye therefore that they which are of faith, the same are the children of Abraham" (Gal. 3:7). This is true of all people, without distinction of ethnicity, social status, gender, or any other distinction (Gal. 3:28). Christ came for the right purpose. He was "made under the law" in order to remove sin, which gives death its sting by virtue of God's broken law (1 Cor. 15:56). Christ was subject to the law as a covenant. Where Adam failed to keep this law for himself and for us, Christ came as the Second Adam in order to justify many: "For as by one man's disobedience many were made sinners, so by the obedience of one shall many be made righteous" (Rom. 5:19). Do you know that the Father sent His Son at the right time, in the right way, and for the right purpose? Is this the bedrock on which you build your hope?

God sent His Son to adopt us (v. 5). Herman Witsius (1636–1708) wrote that God makes us His children by birth, by marriage, and by adoption.[44] We are children by birth through regeneration. We are children by marriage through the Spirit uniting us to the Son. We are children by adoption through God transferring us into His family for Christ's sake. However, there is an obstacle to our adoption by the Father. We must be redeemed from the curse of His law. By nature, we belong to the wrong family. We are children of Satan in relation to sin (John 8:44) and we are children of wrath in relation to God (Eph. 2:3). We must be transferred from the kingdom of darkness into the kingdom of God's dear Son (Col. 1:13) by the new birth (John 3:3), by marriage (Eph. 5:21ff), and by adoption (Rom. 8:15). Though God has only one natural Son, He has many adopted sons and daughters. Christ redeemed those who were "under the law" by being made "under the law," bearing the curse and the penalty of the broken law as a substitute for God's adopted children (Gal. 3:14). We could not be adopted as God's children unless

[44] Herman Witsius, *The Economy of the Covenants Between God and Man* (Grand Rapids, MI: Reformation Heritage Books, 2010), 3.10.9–13 (1:444–446).

sin and Satan no longer had a legal right or claim to us. As adopted children, "we are received into the number, and have a right to all the privileges, of the sons of God."[45] Daughters have the rights belonging to firstborn sons in the divine family as well. We all inherit the entire estate. Have you been redeemed and adopted by God?

God sent His Son to give us the Spirit of His Son (v. 6). John wrote, "Behold, what manner of love the Father has bestowed on us, that we should be called the sons of God: therefore the world does not know us, because it did not know Him. Beloved, now are we the sons of God, and it doth not yet appear what we shall be: but we know that, when He appears, we shall be like Him; for we shall see Him as He is" (1 John 3:1–2). God placed the Spirit of His Son in our hearts. He is the Spirit who filled Christ (Jn. 3:34), who comes to us through Christ (John 15:26), who directs us to Christ (John 16:14), and who makes us like Christ (Rom. 8:28–29). Prayer is the primary expression of having the Spirit of Christ in our hearts (Rom. 8:15, 26–27). He teaches us for whom, what, and how to pray.[46] He also intercedes in our hearts, enabling us to groan inexpressibly with desires for our heavenly Father and those things that please Him. Every Christian has two Almighty intercessors in every simple act of prayer: Christ, who is in heaven, and the Spirit of Christ, who is in our hearts. We receive the promised Spirit through faith (Gal. 3:15). Have you received the Spirit of the Son through faith? Is it your joy and privilege to offer your feeble and broken prayers to God because you come as children to a Father who is able and ready to help you?[47]

Cultivate the Spirit of adoption in your hearts so that you might call God Father in Christ's name.

Study Questions:

1. What does it mean that God sent His Son "in the fullness of time?"
2. How do we become children of God? What is the significance of being treated as firstborn sons?
3. Why is being made like Christ a benefit of the Gospel?

---

[45] *Westminster Shorter Catechism*, question 34.

[46] *Westminster Larger Catechism*, questions 182–185.

[47] *Westminster Shorter Catechism*, question 100.

Chapter Thirteen

The Trinity and Prayer Meetings

"Most assuredly, I say to you, he who believes in Me, the works that I do he will do also; and greater works than these he will do, because I go to My Father. And whatever you ask in My name, that I will do, that the Father may be glorified in the Son. If you ask anything in My name, I will do it." (John 14:12–14)[48]

Many Christians believe that we live in a "day of small things" (Zech. 4:10). Churches are largely in decline in the western world. Their influence on culture as salt and light appears to be fading. However, from God's perspective, we live in a day of great things. Christ has come; He has poured out the Spirit whom He received from the Father (Acts 2:33). He demonstrated this great work on the day of Pentecost in Acts 2. John 14:12–14 anticipated this event by instructing the Church in what to do and how to do it after the outpouring of the Spirit. She would do the same works that Christ had done, (and greater things than these,) and She would accomplish them through prayer in His name. The book of Acts confirms the fact that the Spirit was the mighty engine through which the Church accomplished these things. This text teaches us that a primary concern of the Church in every age should be corporate prayer for the Spirit of God to make the preaching of God's Word effective for the salvation of many people. The text reveals the astonishing truth that preaching is better than miracles, prayer precedes effective preaching, and corporate prayer is better than private prayer.

Those who believe in Christ would do the same works and

---

[48] This material is condensed from Ryan M. McGraw, *How Do Preaching and Corporate Prayer Work Together?, Cultivating Biblical Godliness* (Grand Rapids, MI: Reformation Heritage Books, 2014).

greater things than He had done. The same works refers to apostolic miracles (see verse 11). However great these works were, they were not greater than Christ's miracles. While the apostles raised the dead, Christ raised a man who had been in a tomb for four days. He surpassed every miracle by laying down His own life and taking it up again (John 10:17–18). The Greek text does not indicate that the apostles would do greater miraculous works than Christ did, but that those who believe in Him would do "greater things than these." The book of Acts illustrates what these "greater things" were. After Peter's first sermon (Acts 2), Christ's 120 disciples suddenly became 3,000 (Acts 2:41). Soon the number grew to 5,000 (Acts 4:4) and the Lord was adding to the Church daily such as should be saved (Acts 2:47). This is the only work that Christ did through the Church that was greater than His works in His earthly ministry. The Spirit's task in regenerating souls is comparable in majesty only to the power through which God created the world (2 Cor. 4:6). The "greater things" consist in Spirit-empowered preaching for the conversion of sinners to the Father through Christ. It is to those who believe in Christ only that this promise belongs. Do you believe in Christ? Do you recognize that the Word is effective only through His power? Moreover, do you realize how momentous preaching is? It is the power of God to salvation for all who believe. Do you come to sermons expecting Christ to do something greater than apostolic miracles? Do you rest in Him to do this in your own soul?

Corporate prayer in Christ's name is the means of accomplishing these "greater things." Christ tells us that He will do whatever we ask in His name. The Greek for "you" is plural." As people say in the southern United States, Christ promises to bless whatever "y'all" ask in His name. The book of Acts exemplified the fact that the early Church understood this as a mandate for corporate prayer. Virtually every crisis in the Church was answered with a prayer meeting. When Peter was released from prison under threats from the Jewish leaders not to preach in Christ's name anymore, he did not go to his closet to pray. He went to the corporate prayer meeting (Acts 4:32–24). The church prayed to the Father in Christ's name that He would give the Spirit. They asked Him to give them boldness in preaching and to do miracles in Christ's name (v. 29–30). In other words, they prayed to do the same works that Christ did (miracles) and to do "greater things" (Spirit-empowered preaching). The Father blessed their prayer meeting when the Spirit shook the building tangibly. The result was that the men went out preaching the Word with boldness (v. 31). Acts 4:23–31 is virtually an inspired commentary on John 14:12–14. Prayer meetings are ordinarily the worst attended meeting in the local church today, especially if they do not include a Bible study. This is tantamount to telling the Holy Spirit that His services are not required and that we can carry on fine without Him as long as we keep preaching and studying the Bible. Does our practice match the example set by the early Church? Are we using the means that Christ appointed to see Him do "greater things" than the miracles He performed through the Spirit's power? Do you realize that you are at least as responsible for the sermon through your prayers as the minister is through combining prayer with his studies? Some object that God can hear them just as well in private and that the prayer meeting is superfluous. Would we not do better to lay aside our objections, follow the early Church's example, and lay hold of Christ's promises? To the degree that we prioritize prayer meetings in the local church we show our esteem to the Spirit's work in Gospel preaching. Though the Spirit is sovereign, working when, where, and how He pleases, the widespread neglect of prayer meetings may be one factor in why we see so few conversions in many western churches today.

Make good use of prayer meetings in order to see the Spirit do great things by bringing people to the Father through His Son. Use prayer meetings to undergird the preaching of the Word.

Study Questions:

1. What are "the same works" and the "greater things" that Christ promised to give the Church in this text?
2. Why is the ministry of the Spirit vital to the preaching of the Gospel?
3. What means does Christ give to accomplish the "greater things?" How are you partly responsible for the sermon every week?
4. What should be our attitude toward and expectations from the preaching of the Word?

5. Why are prayer meetings so important? How can you begin prioritizing prayer meetings in your life? How can you help your local congregation begin prayer meetings if you do not have them?

Chapter Fourteen

The Trinity and the Church

"I, therefore, the prisoner of the Lord, beseech you to walk worthy of the calling with which you were called, with all lowliness and gentleness, with longsuffering, bearing with one another in love, endeavoring to keep the unity of the Spirit in the bond of peace. There is one body and one Spirit, just as you were called in one hope of your calling; one Lord, one faith, one baptism; one God and Father of all, who is above all, and through all, and in you all. But to each one of us grace was given according to the measure of Christ's gift. Therefore He says:" When He ascended on high, He led captivity captive, And gave gifts to men." Now this, "He ascended"—what does it mean but that He also first descended into the lower parts of the earth? He who descended is also the One who ascended far above all the heavens, that He might fill all things." (Eph. 4:1–10)

Francis Turretin (1623–1687) wrote, "The Church is the primary work of the Trinity, the object of Christ's mediation and the subject of the application of His benefits."[49] However, it is common to meet people in the United States of America who say that they are Christians, but who add that they have not been to church in years. Some believe that they are born again and that they are members of the "invisible" Church,[50] but they say that they have no use for local churches, either because they have been "burned" too many times

---

[49] Francis Turretin (1623-1687), *Institutes of Elenctic Theology*, ed. James T Dennison, trans. George Musgrave Giger, 3 vols. (Phillipsburg, NJ: P&R Publishing, 1992), 18.1.3; 3:1. These references lists topic, question, and chapter, followed by volume and page number in the translated version of this work.

[50] *Westminster Larger Catechism*, question 64: "The invisible church is the whole number of the elect, that have been, are, or shall be gathered into one under Christ the head."

or because they cannot find a church that meets their standards.[51] The Bible presents a very different picture of the Church. As William Perkins asserted, the Church is "the suburbs of the city of God, and the gate of heaven; and therefore entrance must be made into heaven in and by the Church."[52] The Church is the sphere in which the Father calls the elect to Himself through Christ by the Spirit.

While the term "church" does not appear in Ephesians 4:1-10, it is clearly the Church that is in view here. Christ is head over all things to the Church, which is the fullness of Him who fills all in all (Eph. 1:22-23). The Church is the household of God (Eph. 2:19), the body of Christ (Col. 1:18), and the temple of the Spirit (1 Cor. 3:16). Christ loved the Church and He died for her (Eph. 5:25). This text teaches that the Church reflects the Trinity by expressing unity in diversity.

The Triune God calls the Church to reflect God's unity. God is one (Gal. 3:20). This means not only that there is one God, but also that "we worship one God in trinity and the trinity in unity, neither blending their persons nor dividing their essence."[53] Christ prayed that believers would be one even as He and the Father are one (John 17:21). These truths have bearing on how believers should treat one another. We must walk worthy of our calling in Christ, "with all lowliness and gentleness, with longsuffering, bearing with one another in love, endeavoring to keep the unity of the Spirit in the bond of peace" (Eph. 4:2). The Father answered Christ's prayer. Though we are many, we are one in Christ (Rom. 12:5). This made the disunity of the Corinthians tantamount to blasphemy. Their practices did not reflect the fact that they were together the temple of the Holy Spirit (1 Cor. 3:16). In Christ, we are being built together as living stones into a holy habitation of God in the Spirit (Eph. 2:22; 1 Peter 2:4–6). While Christians will not agree on everything on this side of glory, Paul teaches us that if we must be narrow in our convictions, then we must be broad in our affections as well. We must not only

---

[51] For a biblical treatment of the need to join a local church by vows, see Ryan M. McGraw and Ryan Speck, *Is Church Membership Biblical?* (Grand Rapids, MI: Reformation Heritage Books, 2016).

[52] William Perkins, *A Warning Against the Idolatrie of the Last Times and an Instruction Touching Religious, or Divine Worship*. (Cambridge: Printed by John Legat, 1601), 145.

[53] Adapted from the Athanasian Creed.

believe the right things, but we must hold to our beliefs in the right way. As much as lies in us, we must strive to live peaceably with all men (Rom. 12:18). In doing so, as Manton wrote, "Let us study to imitate the Trinity."[54]

The Triune God calls the Church to reflect God's diversity. The unity of the divine Persons finds expression through their united work. The Church is united in "one body and one Spirit." This flows from the "one hope of your calling." There is "one Lord," Jesus Christ, who is the ground of our common faith, which is signified and sealed in our "one baptism." The one God and Father, who is above all, and through all, and in us all, unites all believers under His authority. In agreement with what we have seen above, these descriptions reflect the appropriate work of each divine Person. The Spirit makes the Church one through applying Christ's work to us in our effectual calling. The Son makes the Church one in faith by purchasing us through his blood. The Father makes the Church one through bringing the plan of redemption to fruition in Christ by the Spirit. As the work of each divine Person functions in the single operation of God, so the diverse services of believers share the single goal of profiting the Church. This is why James Bannerman (1807–1868) wrote, "According to the arrangement of God, the Christian is more of a Christian in society than alone, and more in the enjoyment of privileges of a spiritual kind when he shares them with others, than when he possesses them apart."[55]

The Triune God gifts the Church to serve Him through Christ. The idea that all men are created equal in the sight of God can be misleading. While we are equal in value as human beings, we are not equal in gifts and abilities. Contrary to popular misconceptions, our children cannot be anything that they want to be. Not everyone is gifted to be President of the United States. Paul is stressing that in the realm of the Church, not only is there nothing wrong with that fact, but we possess different abilities by God's design. When

---

[54] Manton, *The Complete Works*, 11:333.

[55] James Bannerman, *The Church of Christ: A Treatise on the Nature, Powers, Ordinances, Discipline, and Government of the Christian Church* (Birmingham, AL: Solid Ground Christian Books, 2009), 1:91.

Christ ascended into heaven, He gave gifts to men. This draws from the imagery of Psalm 68, in which the Lord as the conquering King received gifts from His subjects (v. 18) and distributed His wealth among His followers (v. 19). Christ descended to "the lowest parts of the earth" in His incarnation, culminating with His death and burial. Christ "ascended far above the heavens" following His resurrection. As we saw above, He received the Spirit from the Father that He might pour out His Spirit on the Church. We will consider the diversity of His gifts in the next chapter. It is important to note here that He did not give diverse gifts to His people for their own benefit. It must be for the edification of the Church that we seek to excel in using our gifts (1 Cor. 14:12). Whether you have one talent, three talents, or five talents, you must use your talents to serve rather than to be served. Faithfulness is more important than fruitfulness in Christ's service. Do you seek recognition in the Church? Are you upset because your church has not recognized that you should serve as an officer? How different would our attitudes toward our gifts be if we remembered their purposes of reflecting the glory of the Triune God and promoting the unity of the Church?

If you neglect or despise the Church of God, then you are dishonoring Christ. As Bannerman noted, "A solitary Christian is worse than a contradiction, he is an anomaly, standing out against the express institution of God, which has appointed the fellowship of believers in one Church, and has made provision in its outward ordinances for its union and edification."[56] Positively, live in communion with other believers as you learn to "imitate the Trinity."

Study Questions:

1. Why is the Church so important in Scripture? What should our attitude be towards the local church?
2. How does our unity and diversity in the Church reflect the Triune God? What practical implications does this have for our interaction with fellow believers in the Church?
3. What are the purposes of spiritual gifts? How and why should we exercise our gifts in the Church?

---

[56] Bannerman, *The Church of Christ*, 1:20–21.

Chapter Fifteen

The Trinity and Spiritual Gifts

"And He Himself gave some to be apostles, some prophets, some evangelists, and some pastors and teachers, for the equipping of the saints for the work of ministry, for the edifying of the body of Christ, till we all come to the unity of the faith and of the knowledge of the Son of God, to a perfect man, to the measure of the stature of the fullness of Christ; that we should no longer be children, tossed to and fro and carried about with every wind of doctrine, by the trickery of men, in the cunning craftiness of deceitful plotting, but, speaking the truth in love, may grow up in all things into Him who is the head—Christ—from whom the whole body, joined and knit together by what every joint supplies, according to the effective working by which every part does its share, causes growth of the body for the edifying of itself in love." (Eph. 4:11–16)

How should we think about spiritual gifts? Spiritual gifts divided the Corinthian church even though the Lord gave them to unite believers in serving Christ through serving one another (1 Cor. 12:1–14). Christians can become more preoccupied with identifying their particular gifts (even taking surveys to help them do so) than they are with obeying God's commands through serving others. Spiritual gifts reflect the generosity of the Triune God to us. We should use them generously by imitating Him as His children. We often discover and develop gifts through using them. Paul helps us do this by drawing our attention to broader principles. The Father's greatest gift to us was His Son (Rom. 8:32). The Son's "great legacy" to us is the Holy Spirit (John 20:22).[57] Among other things, the Spirit blesses us with sound doctrine and with the power to receive it for our salvation. This text teaches us that Christ gave the Church

[57] Owen, *Pneumatalogia*, *Works*, 3:156.

ministers of the Word for the instruction and maturity of the body of Christ. Though the Father and the Spirit are not mentioned here explicitly, these "gifts" promote the proper functioning of all other gifts in the Church as believers use them for God's glory by the Spirit. Christ singled out church officers as preeminent gifts to the Church. These officers are actually the only gifts mentioned in this list. What all five categories of officers have in common is their teaching function and that they all reflect Christ's Prophetic office. Christ possesses all spiritual gifts and all spiritual offices. He received the Spirit without measure (John 3:34) so that He might give to each of us a measure of grace (Eph. 4:7; see Rom. 12:3 for the same subject). He is "the Apostle and High Priest of our confession" (Heb. 3:1). He is the Prophet like Moses and the greatest Prophet who ever lived (Deut. 18:15; Acts 3:22). He is the Evangelist par excellence who seeks and saves the lost (Luke 19:10). He is the Great Shepherd (pastor) and overseer of our souls (John 10:11; 1 Peter 2:25). He is the "good teacher" (Luke 18:18) who declares the Father to us (John 1:18).

The teaching offices listed here continue Christ's office as Prophet in the Church. The Apostles and Prophets laid the foundation of the Church in Christ through their preaching and writings (Eph. 2:20; 1 Cor. 3:11). These offices were temporary, passing away with the closing the New Testament canon.[58] There is no provision for their successors such as we have with elders and deacons (1 Tim. 3:1–13) and no one can any longer meet apostolic qualifications (Acts 2:21–22).[59] While the definition of "Evangelists" is debated, most Reformed authors have taught that this was an office that passed away with the Apostles since such men were assistants to the Apostles. However, all assert the duty to continue the work of evan-

[58] For arguments in favor of this position, see, Walter J. Chantry, *Signs of the Apostles: Observations on Pentecostalism Old and New* (Edinburgh; Carlisle, Pa.: Banner of Truth Trust, 1976); Richard B. Gaffin, *Perspectives on Pentecost: Studies in New Testament Teaching on the Gifts of the Holy Spirit* (Phillipsburg, NJ: P&R Pub. Co., 1979); O. Palmer Robertson, *The Final Word: A Biblical Response to the Case for Tongues and Prophecy Today* (Edinburgh: Banner of Truth, 1993).

[59] See Owen, *Works*, 15:249 who observes that becoming an apostle required: 1. An immediate call from Christ, 2. extraordinary gifts, 3. divine inspiration, and 4. extensive commission to serve in authority over the whole Church.

gelism. If the first three categories of officers included extraordinary ministers of the Word, pastors and teachers are ordinary ministers of the Word, who continue to serve the Church today.[60] This stresses the fact that one of the primary concerns of the ascended Christ is to secure sound teaching in the Church through the ministry of the Word through faithful teaching officers. This does not mean that other gifts or offices are unimportant. However, it should make us ask, "Do we value the ministry of the Word as Christ does?"

Positively, Christ designed church officers to promote unity and maturity in the faith. Paul stated the function of teaching offices in the Church both positively and negatively. Through sound teaching from Scripture, they should equip the saints for ministry and so edify the body of Christ. By doing so, they promote the unity in diversity urged in light of the Trinity in verses 1-6. To be a perfect man means to be a mature man, like Noah, who was "a just man and perfect in his generations" (Gen. 6:9). Yet the "perfect man" here refers to the corporate growth of the entire Church as they sit together under sound preaching and grow up in Christ. When the Church stands up to its full height in glory, it will reach to the measure of the fullness of the stature of Christ. In the meantime, we are like growing children who hope to be as tall as their fathers one day. Christ designed church officers ultimately to promote love among believers. 1 Corinthians 16:13–14 summarizes this goal well: "Watch, stand fast in the faith, be brave, be strong. Let all that you do be done with love."

Negatively, sound teachers who teach sound doctrine help prevent us from being tossed to and fro by every wind of doctrine. This means that pastors and teachers should spend much time in the study, on their knees in fervent prayer. They should be precise and discerning men. False doctrine is often subtle. If false teaching did not possess some measure of truth, then it would not appeal to anyone. False prophets "secretly bring in destructive heresies" (2 Peter 2:1) and true teachers help expose them. Yet true teachers must

[60] Owen noted helpfully that there is always some parallel between the extraordinary gifts of the Spirit and the ordinary gifts of the Spirit. So, in this case, extraordinary ministers of the Word are replaced by ordinary ministers of the Word. Owen, *Works*, 4:516.

also speak the truth in love. They must be gentle to all and not quarrelsome (2 Tim. 2:24). There are few worse signs in a Christian preacher than loving to pick theological fights, notwithstanding his soundness in faith otherwise. Such teaching enables the Church to be knit together, to serve one another, and to edify itself in love. If we adopt the attitude that me on my island with my Bible (and maybe with my family in a "home church") are enough, then we should not be surprised if we are unstable in the faith and end up as ships at sea without a rudder.

I am reminded of a man who decided to leave the church and stay home to worship God with his wife. In their course of Bible reading in family worship, the man came to this passage and told his wife, "This is sinful. We need to be in church." Let us value the ministry of the Word as Christ does. Let us learn to use Christ's gifts by the Spirit to the glory of the Father.

Study Questions:

1. Why do spiritual gifts often divide Christians? How can we avoid this pitfall?
2. What gifts does Christ promise to give in this text? How are they important to the vitality and health of the Church?
3. Why should your minister spend much time in the study? How can you help promote good study habits in your minister as a faithful church member? In what ways can you hinder his study time unnecessarily?
4. What are the purposes of the teaching ministry of the Church? How does this help the Church? Why does this imply that we need to be part of a local congregation?

Chapter Sixteen
The Trinity and Worship

"Jesus said to her, "Woman, believe Me, the hour is coming when you will neither on this mountain, nor in Jerusalem, worship the Father. You worship what you do not know; we know what we worship, for salvation is of the Jews. But the hour is coming, and now is, when the true worshipers will worship the Father in spirit and truth; for the Father is seeking such to worship Him. God is Spirit, and those who worship Him must worship in spirit and truth." (John 4:21–24)

Do we share the Father's goals for preaching? The Gospel is about the glory of God. It is not primarily about receiving benefits, but about receiving Christ and in Him the benefits of redemption. Unless love for Christ sustains us in Christian life and ministry, our faith will fail us under trial by losing sight of its grand object. The centrality of God's glory in Christ in the Gospel demands the centrality of worship under the Gospel. Since the Triune God is the object of worship, then the Gospel and the worship that the Gospel produces is Trinitarian. This affects gospel preaching in two ways. Ministers must preach a Trinitarian Gospel, and they must preach a Gospel that presents worshiping the Triune God as its primary goal. John 4:21–24 teaches us that the Father's goal in gospel preaching is to seek those who will worship Him in Spirit and in truth.

The Father is seeking worshipers. The fact that the Father is seeking worshipers lies at the heart of the Gospel message. He represents here the honor of the entire Godhead. Jesus' conversation with the Samaritan woman occurred at the foot of Mount Gerizim. The heart of the disagreement between Jews and Gentiles respected the true manner of worshiping the true God. This revolved around the question of whether Mount Sinai our Mount Gerizim was the divinely appointed place for public worship (Jn. 4:20). When Jesus proved to the woman that He was a true Prophet sent from God by telling her all that she ever did (v. 16–19, 29), she knew that He could resolve the debate over worship that so divided Jews and Samarians (v. 20). She did not change the subject. She asked the most important question of all, which was, and remains, how should people worship God? The Father sent Christ to save sinners (Matt. 18:11; Luke 19:10) and Christ sends His Church to spread the Gospel (Matt. 29:18–20) because the Father is seeking true worshipers. Worship is the goal of God's plan of salvation. God designed us to glorify Him and enjoy Him forever.[61] Let worshiping the Father serve as the heart of your Christian life and as the lifeblood of your evangelism.

We must worship the Father in Spirit. God is a spiritual being ("God is a Spirit") who requires spiritual worship ("those who worship Him must worship in Spirit"). As Stephen Charnock wrote, "His being a spirit declares what He is, His other perfections declare what kind of spirit He is."[62] God's spiritual essence led Paul to say, "He cannot be served with the works of men's hands" (Acts 17:29, etc.). This means that we must worship the God, who is spirit, in the Holy Spirit. John consistently used the term "Spirit" to refer to the third Person in the Trinity.[63] This is true particularly in John 14–16, where Jesus treated the Spirit's work in detail. The Spirit is the author of the new birth (John 3:3–5). He changes our hearts and writes God's Law on them (Jer. 31:33; Ezek. 36:26). Worshiping the Father in Spirit demands worshiping Him with renewed affections. As Charnock noted, "The heart must first be cast into the mould of the Gospel, before it can perform a worship required by the Gospel."[64] God does not accept the worship of those who draw near to Him with their lips while their hearts are far from Him (Matt. 15:8;

---

[61] *Westminster Shorter Catechism*, question 1.

[62] Stephen Charnock, *Several Discourses Upon the Existence and Attributes of God by That Late Eminent Minister of Christ, Mr. Stephen Charnocke, B.D. and Sometimes Fellow of New-Colledge in Oxon* (London: Printed for D. Newman, T. Cockerill, Benj. Griffin, T. Simmons, and Benj. Alsop. And are to be sold by Michael Hide Bookseller in Exon, 1682), 131.

[63] Letham, *The Holy Trinity*, 415.

[64] Charnock, *Existence and Attributes of God*, 142.

Is. 29:13). Only the pure in heart shall see God (Matt. 5:8). This is true when we worship in this life as well as in the life to come. In order to worship God properly, we must meditate on those truths of Scripture that will stir up our affections for Him in worship. We must pray for and trust in the blessing of the Spirit of God so that we may worship the Father suitably.

We must worship the Father in truth. Jesus Christ is the way, the truth, and the life. No one comes to the Father except through Him (John 14:6. See 1:9, 14, 17). Worshiping the Father "in truth" means approaching Him in Christ's name (John 17:3; 1 Tim. 2:5). Christ governs us by His Word and Spirit (John 16:3 with 1 John 2:20, 27). His office as King requires us to worship Him according to His Word alone (Deut. 12:29-32). We must come to the Father through Christ, who is full of grace and truth (John 1:14). We must govern how we approach the Father according to Christ's revealed will (Col. 2:23). We must do all that God commands us to do in worship, neither adding to it nor taking away from it (Deut. 12:29-32). Adding elements to our worship that Christ has not commanded in that context, such as dance and drama, inhibits worshiping in Spirit and in truth. We must dance, sleep, and go to war for God's glory, but we must also worship him in the sanctuary (Ps. 149). Sleeping, warfare, and dancing are appropriate outside of the sanctuary, but bringing them into the sanctuary would create a bizarre and confused service. Whether we eat or drink or whatever we do we must do all things to God's glory, giving thanks to Him through Christ (1 Cor. 10:30; Col. 3:17). We can only present our bodies as living sacrifices to God, which is our spiritual worship (Rom. 12:1–2), by learning how to serve Him appropriately in every context in life. We must learn to do the right things, in the right way, and at the right time. Conversely, what we do on the Sabbath in worship trains us how to honor God in all other areas of life.[65]

Biblical worship is simple in its external form. Its primary ele-

[65] For a treatment of the Sabbath in relation to Christian living in general, see Ryan M. McGraw, *The Day of Worship: Reassessing the Christian Life in Light of the Sabbath* (Grand Rapids, MI: Reformation Heritage Books, 2011).

ments are preaching and reading the Bible, singing, and praying, with the sacraments serving as the visible Word of God.[66] Its focus is spiritual communion with the God who is Spirit. If we do not strive to worship in truth, then we cannot worship in Spirit adequately. Just as the Spirit proceeds from the Father through the Son (John 14:26; 15:26), so the work of the Spirit is married to Christ, who is the eternal Word of God and the highest revelation of the Father (John 1:1–5, 18). Christ is the true prophet who testified of Himself by His Spirit in all of Scripture (1 Peter 1:10–12). Worship the Father in truth by worshiping Him through Christ according to Scripture. Christ's conversation with the woman at the well revolved around public worship. We must worship God by obeying Him in every area of life (Rom. 12:1–2). Yet when we come to public worship with the Church of God, we enter God's special presence and experience His special blessing (Ps. 100:4). Public worship is where the Triune God is present most frequently and most powerfully with His people. We should value it and love it to God's glory.

Worship the Father in Spirit and in Truth.

Study Questions:

1. What is the Father seeking through gospel preaching? What are the implications of this for preaching and for personal evangelism?
2. What does it mean that God is a Spirit?
3. What does it mean to worship God in Spirit? What are the practical implications of this truth as we prepare for public worship?
4. What does it mean to worship God in truth? How should this affect the way in which we worship God?
5. How should we distinguish what we do in public worship from what we do to God's glory in the rest of life?

---

[66] For a classic treatment of these elements of biblical worship, see Jeremiah Burroughs, *Gospel-Worship, Or, the Right Manner of Sanctifying the Name of God in General and Particularly in These Three Great Ordinances, Viz. 1. Hearing of the Word, 2. Receiving the Lords Supper, 3. Prayer* (London: Printed by Peter Cole, 1658).

Chapter Seventeen

The Trinity and the Gospel Ministry

"Blessed be the God and Father of our Lord Jesus Christ, the Father of mercies and God of all comfort, who comforts us in all our tribulation, that we may be able to comfort those who are in any trouble, with the comfort with which we ourselves are comforted by God. For as the sufferings of Christ abound in us, so our consolation also abounds through Christ. Now if we are afflicted, it is for your consolation and salvation, which is effective for enduring the same sufferings which we also suffer. Or if we are comforted, it is for your consolation and salvation. And our hope for you is steadfast, because we know that as you are partakers of the sufferings, so also you will partake of the consolation ... "For the Son of God, Jesus Christ, who was preached among you by us—by me and Silas and Timothy—was not "Yes" and "No," but in him it has always been "Yes." For no matter how many promises God has made, they are "Yes" in Christ. And so through him the "Amen" is spoken by us to the glory of God. Now it is God who makes both us and you stand firm in Christ. He anointed us, set his seal of ownership on us, and put his Spirit in our hearts as a deposit, guaranteeing what is to come." (2 Cor. 1:3–7, 19–22)

Christ appointed a teaching ministry in order to bless His Church (Eph. 4:11–14). Just as Christ suffered for the salvation of the Church, so Christian ministers will suffer hardship as good soldiers of Christ (2 Tim. 2:3). There is no such thing as a Christian without trials and affliction. In the world we will have tribulation (John 16:33). Those whom Christ makes pre-eminent in usefulness, He makes pre-eminent in suffering. The Father's comforts keep step with the trials of His servants who then comfort the Church with the comforts that they receive. 2 Corinthians 1 teaches that the Triune God comforts a suffering Church through suffering servants whom He comforts in all of their afflictions.

The Father comforts His ministers and those who belong to His Church through them. He is the Father of mercies and the God of all comfort. His comforts correspond to the trials of His servants. Paul valued God's compassion and comfort more deeply because of his great affliction. 2 Corinthians is concerned with Paul's credentials as a true apostle of Jesus Christ. He defended his office by appealing to God's call and the evidences of that call in performing the "signs of an apostle" (2 Cor. 12:12), namely miracles.[67] In addition, he vindicated his ministry by appealing to the nature of his work. This makes 2 Corinthians uniquely suited to teach us about the work and purpose of the Christian ministry. Paul and other Gospel ministers are the first objects of the Father's comforting work in this text. Yet God gives a wealth of comfort to His ministers so that they might enrich others through their teaching and example. Ministers and Church members will never share every experience of affliction in common. Even though we do not have the same trials, we all share in the same comforts. If you are a minister, then trust in the Father to minister to the Church through your trials, encouragements, preaching, prayers and exhortations.

The Father comforts believers through His ministers in His Son. They share in Christ's sufferings and they share in His comforts (2 Cor. 1:5). Christ is in heaven and His enemies are on earth. While His bodily presence is lacking, an unbelieving world often takes out their animosity toward Christ on His people and His ministers in particular. God has designed this to work for the good and the salvation of His people (Col. 1:24). Christ is always faithful in doing this work. While Paul and we cannot make definite plans without recognizing that God can overrule them (2 Cor. 1:17–18), God's promises to believers in Christ are certain (v. 19). Christ is the sum and the substance of all of God's promises and they are wrapped up in Him (v. 20). This means that Jesus Christ should be the sum and substance of the Christian ministry. The Father administers His comforts to believers through Christ and He administers none apart

---

[67] See Chantry, *Signs of the Apostles*.

from Him. This does not require a theory of preaching Christ that ministers should impose on every sermon. It requires ministers primarily to experience the power of the Father's comforts through His promises in Christ so that these experiences inevitably saturate their sermons. Pray that God would bless your minister with experiencing the comforts of the Father's promises in Christ and that the Spirit would enable Him to help you experience the same things.

The Father comforts believers by His Spirit (2 Cor. 1:21–22). The Father establishes believers in their union with Christ. He does so by anointing them. The Holy Spirit is the anointing of the Father through Christ, the Holy One (1 John 2:20, 27). Christ anoints believers with the Spirit and the Spirit is the substance of their anointing. He is also God's seal on believers (v. 22). Sealing is not merely something that the Spirit does to believers. He is the seal that the Father has set upon believers. Just as a king placed his seal on a document, assuring all who saw it that it belonged to him and represented his will, so the Spirit dwelling in the hearts of believers seals the fact that they belong to the Father through the Son. The Spirit is a down payment of our inheritance in heaven as well. A down payment is more than a pledge. A pledge is a promise to pay more. As we have seen above, a down payment is partial ownership at present. To the degree that we cultivate fellowship with the Holy Spirit, we have already begun to enjoy the joys of heaven. As Owen wrote, "So much as we have of the Spirit, so much we have of heaven in its perfect enjoyment, and so much evidence of its future fullness."[68] Pray for more of the anointing of the Spirit on your pastor's ministry. Trust in the Father who has set His seal on you and begin to enjoy the comforts of heaven by loving and honoring the Holy Spirit in your life.

A world full of sin is a world full of suffering. While we do not always suffer for our personal sins, all suffering stems from the presence of sin in ourselves, in others, and in our world. Ministers should not despair when they suffer affliction in their ministries or for their ministries. The Father will comfort them through His Son by His

[68] Owen, *Communion with God*, *Works*, 2:246.

Spirit in all of their trials. Ministers are not useful to the Church merely because they suffer. Even non-Christians achieve this. They are useful when they experience the comforts of communion with the Triune God and when God enables them to administer these comforts to others.

Seek the comforts of the Triune God as a fruit of the Gospel ministry.

Study Questions:

1. How is suffering related to Christian ministry? Why is this significant for all believers?
2. How should we receive the Father's comforts through the Christian ministry, even when our ministers have not experienced the same trials that we have?
3. How does the Father comfort us in trials through His Son and by His Spirit?
4. How are sin and suffering related?

Chapter Eighteen

The Trinity and Baptism

"Go therefore, and teach all nations, baptizing them in the name of the Father, and of the Son, and of the Holy Ghost." (*Matt.* 28:19)

Baptism is our introduction into the visible Church on earth.[69] It stands at the inception of the Christian life. Every Christian must be baptized because Christ instituted baptism, because it is a divine command (Acts 2:38), and because it is a visible sign and seal of our union with Christ in His person and in His work. Christ is central to our salvation, but when we are baptized, we are not only baptized into Christ's name (Acts 2:38), but into the name of all three Persons in the Trinity. This is because in baptism, all three Persons in the Godhead dedicate us to themselves and to the care of their saving work. Baptism brings us under the umbrella of the great New Testament "name" of God, which in our text is Father, Son, and Holy Spirit.[70] Stressing the saving work of each divine Person particularly and of the entire Godhead generally highlights the comforts that you should receive from your baptism as you reflect upon it through faith.

We are baptized into the name of God the Father because we belong to Him from eternity past (Eph. 1:3; John 17). When we think

[69] *Westminster Confession of Faith*, 28:1 states, "Baptism is a sacrament of the New Testament, ordained by Jesus Christ, not only for the solemn admission of the party baptized into the visible Church; but also to be unto him a sign and seal of the covenant of grace, of his ingrafting into Christ, of regeneration, of remission of sins, and of his giving up unto God, through Jesus Christ, to walk in the newness of life. Which sacrament is, by Christ's own appointment, to be continued in His Church until the end of the world."

[70] For the meaning of God's name in Baptism, see J. V. Fesko, *Word, Water, and Spirit: A Reformed Perspective on Baptism* (Grand Rapids, MI: Reformation Heritage Books, 2010), chapter 13.

of our baptism, we should see the Father's eternal love embodied in an outward sign. Our baptism proclaims to us that it is He who so loved us that He gave us His only begotten Son (John 3:16). When we are consumed with the dark shadows of our sin and guilt, then the Father's promise in our baptism should shine upon our souls as a ray of light. Is it not too easy to act as though the Son is a loving and willing Savior, but to think that the Father must somehow be persuaded to love us? If the Father did not intend you to be assured of His everlasting love, then why did the Son command you to be baptized into His name? As Owen wrote,

> "If the love of a Father will not make a child delight in him, what will? Put this to the venture: exercise your thoughts upon this very thing, the eternal, free, and fruitful love of the Father, and see if your hearts be not wrought upon to delight in him. I dare boldly say, believers will find it as thriving a course as ever they pitched upon in their lives. Sit down a little at the fountain, and you will quickly have a farther discovery of the sweetness of the streams. You who have run from him, will not be able, after a while, to keep at a distance for a moment."[71]

Look to your baptism to assure you of the Father's love.

The Son stands at the center of our salvation. As we have seen above, in the works of God, Christ is like a great jewel that stands at the center of a treasure room. The luster of this jewel is so great that it outshines all of the rest of the treasure in the room. However, this analogy does not undermine the importance of the treasure, for what backdrop could be more suitable for such a great jewel? This is likely why the apostles in the book of Acts used the shorthand formula of being baptized "in the name of Jesus."[72] The apostles did not baptize people contrary to Christ's chosen formula in the Great Commission. Instead, baptizing in Christ's name highlights Christ's

---

[71] Owen, *Communion with God*, *Works*, 2:36.

[72] Fesko, *Word, Water, and Spirit*, 313: "While the Triune formula is not explicitly stated, it is materially present, in that God the Father sends the Son who pours out the Spirit. Moreover, the redemption-seeking crowd called on the name of the Lord, Yahweh, in the name of Jesus."

work as central to the saving work of the entire Trinity. In Christ you see the Father's eternal love reflected to you as in a mirror. In the waters of baptism, Christ's work is reflected to you in a visible sign and seal. Baptism is not a savior, but baptism directs you to the true Savior. In baptism, Christ shows you visibly that His blood must wash your body and your soul from your sin and that you must be identified with Him in His death and His resurrection (Rom. 6:1–4). When you witness a baptism, renew your commitment to Christ in faith and repentance.[73]

As we have seen, the Holy Spirit is the bond of communion between your soul and the entire Godhead (2 Cor. 13:14). Baptism, therefore, signifies that without His work you could not embrace either the Father or the Son. Baptism points to the washing of regeneration (Titus 3:3–5). Just as baptism is your inception into the visible Church, so the Spirit, who works in changing your heart, is the source of your faith (Eph. 2:10) and of your inception into fellowship with God. The Spirit seals you for the day of redemption by applying to you the benefits of salvation (Eph. 1:13; 4:30). Similarly,

---

[73] To paraphrase the Dutch theologian, Peter van Mastricht (1630–1706), at baptism you should: (1) Acknowledge the corruption of your nature and sin. Receive baptism as the washing of regeneration and renovation of the Spirit without which no one can see the kingdom of God. (2) Give thanks to God for the washing of regeneration in the blood of Christ and the Holy Spirit who is purifying us, which things are sealed in baptism. (3) Put off more and more the body of sinful flesh because in baptism we have died to sin. (4) Walk in newness of life in the renovation of the Spirit. (5) Cultivate communion with the church into which by baptism you have been planted. (6) Pursue first of all actual spiritual union with Christ, whom you have put on in baptism (Gal. 3:27). (7) Persevere in sound doctrine, into which you have been baptized (Acts 2:41–42). (8) Hold fast to the promises of the covenant, which are held forth in baptism by which we renounce Satan, the sin of the world, and our own sins, committing ourselves wholly to God. God is faithful to keep the promises of his covenant (2 Cor. 1:20). (9) Be assured of the remission of our sins, whose sign and seals is held forth in baptism. (10) Long for the Holy Supper so that you may be nourished and confirmed in the grace of the covenant. (11) Keep whatsoever Christ commands faithfully. Peter van Mastricht, *Theoretico-Practica Theologia. Qua, Per Singula Capita Theologica, Pars Exegetica, Dogmatica, Elenchtica & Practica, Perpetua Successione Conjugantur (Trajecti ad Rhenum, & Amstelodami: Sumptibus Societatis*, 1715), 927–928.

He makes the outward sign of baptism a seal of the saving work of God in your heart.[74] In this way, the Spirit pursues and produces the assurance of your salvation. Let baptism instill confidence in you that the Holy Spirit can make you holy as Christ is holy (1 John 3:1-2) and that He can perfect you in holiness in glory.

Baptism is an implicit confession that you cannot be saved without the work of all three divine Persons. Baptism also signifies that you have been redeemed for the glory of the one true and living God. Your baptism means that you must obey the Father in His authority as Lord of the household of God. If He is a Father, then where is His reverence? (Mal. 1:6). Baptism proclaims that you must rest in the Son who has kept the law of the Father, which you have broken in your sin and rebellion. Baptism indicates that by the power of the Holy Spirit you have the ability to fulfill your obligations to obey God. Look to baptism as a visible preaching of the Gospel, since baptism drives you inescapably to the saving work of the Triune God.

Every time you witness a baptism, let your baptism drive you to depend upon the saving work of the entire Trinity.

Study Questions:

1. How does baptism proclaim the Gospel to us? How does this relate to the work of all three divine Persons?
2. Why do many Christians have hard thoughts about the Father? How does baptism teach us to regard the Father?
3. If Christ taught us to baptize in the name of the Triune God, then why does the Book of Acts record baptism in the name of Christ? How are these things related and why are they significant for Christian living?
4. How does baptism relate to the Church? What implications does this have for our membership and participation in local churches?
5. What should we do when we observe the sacrament of Baptism being administered to others? Are we merely spectators?

---

[74] Mastricht virtually equates the seal in the sacrament with receiving the thing signified in baptism. The seal is the application of the signified grace received through faith. Ibid, 909.

Chapter Nineteen

The Trinity and the Lord's Supper

"Now there are diversities of gifts, but the same Spirit. And there are differences of administrations, but the same Lord. And there are diversities of operations, but it is the same God who works all in all.... For as the body is one, and hath many members, and all the members of that one body, being many, are one body: so also is Christ. For by one Spirit are we all baptized into one body, whether Jews or Gentiles, whether bond or free; and have been all made to drink into one Spirit." (1 Cor. 12:4–6, 12–13)

The sacraments are the visible Word of God.[75] They reflect the nature of God's work in the Church through the Gospel. The words of Scripture give them their meaning and saving power in those who receive them by faith. They represent visibly what God has promised in relation to them. This means that in the Lord's Supper, the Triune God represents what He does in redemption through visible signs and seals of the covenant of grace. 1 Corinthians 12:13 likely alludes to both sacraments: we are baptized into one body and we drink of one Spirit. The remedy to the disunity of the Corinthian church was their common union and communion with their God. The sacraments were visible signs and seals of their union and communion with God and with each other. Paul designed such exhortations to press the Corinthian believers to exercise their spiritual gifts in a way that glorified God and edified the entire Church. This agrees with the pattern seen above in Ephesians 4. In the Lord's Supper, all drink of one Spirit, to the glory of God through faith in Christ.

The Triune God both unites believers and distinguishes them from each other (1 Cor. 12:4–11). Understanding the nature of

---

[75] "A sacrament is defined most briefly as a sign and seal of the covenant of grace." [Sacramentum brevissime definitur: signum et sigillum foederis gratiae]. Mastricht, *Theoretico-Practica Theologia*, 908.

God's work among believers enables us to understand what the Lord's Supper signifies and seals. In the context, Paul argued that believers have varieties of gifts, service, and activities. The unity and diversity among believers is grounded in the unity and diversity within the Godhead, though the emphasis falls here on unity rather than on diversity. Verses 4–6 describe our diverse gifts in relation to the same Spirit, the same Lord, and the same God. The Spirit unites believers in the confession that Christ is Lord (v. 3–4). Christ is the only Lord and Head of the Church, to whom all the members are subject (v. 5). The Father equips each believer to serve the good of the entire Church (v. 6). This text places special emphasis on the work of the Holy Spirit (v. 7–11). This emphasis reflects His work in the application of redemption, to which spiritual gifts are related closely and of which the sacraments are seals. He gives gifts to all church members for the good of the entire Church (v. 7). This is the means by which the Father fulfills His work of equipping and empowering believers. He gives wisdom, knowledge, faith, healings, miracles, prophecies, discernment, speaking in tongues, and interpretation (v. 8–10). While it is beyond the scope of this chapter to address this issue, some of these gifts were temporary.[76] All of them have parallels in ordinary gifts. The Spirit as the common source of these diverse gifts argues for the unity of service in the Church (v. 11). We must base our service to the Church on the nature of the Triune God's work in saving us. Using our gifts to serve ourselves instead of the Lord is sure sign that we have lost sight of the glory of God. Think of the Church in terms of service to triune God rather than merely in terms of using your gifts.

The Lord's Supper represents the unity and diversity of the Church in relation to the Triune God. All kinds of people—Jews, Greeks, slave, and free—are baptized into one body (v. 13). It is the Spirit who plants them into the Church by uniting them to Christ by faith. God has designed both sacraments to signify and seal the work that God is doing in believers. As a sign, Baptism points to

---

[76] See references to the literature on this subject above in connection to extraordinary offices in relation to Ephesians 4. These two issues stand or fall together.

identification and incorporation into one body. This involves union and communion with Christ and with the Church, which is His mystical body. The Lord's Supper as a sign points, in this passage, to drinking from one Spirit, who is within us a fountain of living water (John 7:37). As seals, both sacraments assure believers of the Father's promises to them as individuals and to them collectively as the body of Christ. The work of all three divine Persons makes the Lord's Supper a glorious sign and seal of the covenant. The Supper is particularly a sign and seal of drinking into one Spirit. It involves communion with Christ (1 Cor. 10–11) and feeding on Him through faith (John 6:53, 56). Drinking of one Spirit means that all believers are filled and refreshed through the same living waters. As Richard Sibbes (1677–1635) observed, "The Spirit of the Father and the Son must discover the love of the Father to us in his Son."[77] The Father displays His love in spreading this feast before us. He gave His Son and sent the Spirit. He empowers us to believe in Christ and to serve Him through the Spirit. Though the sacrament is for individual believers, believers cannot observe it individually. We can no more divide the Persons of the Godhead than we can abstract the sacraments from the corporate body of the Church. Like Baptism, the Lord's Supper directs you back to the saving work of the Trinity. See the Gospel preached in the sacrament and believe it. Receive Christ in the sacrament through faith and receive one another in love.

May the Lord's Supper direct you to love and serve one another as you love and serve the Triune God.

Study Questions:

1. How do sacraments relate to the Word of God?
2. What does the Lord's Supper signify and seal? How does this relate to our relationship with other believers?
3. Why is it inappropriate to observe the Lord's Supper in private?

[77] Richard Sibbes, *The Complete Works of Richard Sibbes*, 7 vols. (Edinburgh: James Nichols, 1862), 4:329.

CONCLUSION

Chapter Twenty

The Blessing of the Triune God

"All the saints salute you. The grace of the Lord Jesus Christ, and the love of God, and the communion of the Holy Ghost, be with you all. Amen." (2 Cor. 13:13–14)

A benediction is a proclamation of blessing from the Triune God to His people. It is not a prayer. It is a promise that the Spirit of God makes effective when we receive it by faith. When the priests pronounced a blessing in Numbers 6:23–26, God said that He would place His name upon His people and that He would bless them as a result. Churches often omit benedictions by replacing them with doxologies. A doxology is a blessing from the people to God. It begins with words such as, "To Him who is able . . ." (Jude 24). Benedictions take the form of exhortations, but since they come from God, we should receive them by faith as the Triune God "speaks well" to His people. The benediction at the close of 2 Corinthians is explicitly Trinitarian. The message conveyed by this benediction is that the Triune God Himself is the blessing of His people.

This benediction is couched in terms of the presence of the God of love and peace with His people (2 Cor. 13:11). The promise of God's presence is couched in response to a string of five imperatives in the text. As we rejoice in the Lord ("farewell" is the Greek imperative for "rejoice"), aim for restoration among one another, comfort one another, agree with one another, and live in peace, then the God of love and peace will continue with us. While God does not bless His people on the ground of their obedience, yet He blesses His people in their obedience and for their obedience. Fathers do not love their children because their children obey them. They love them because they are their children. Nevertheless, when children disobey, a faithful father will discipline them and, when they obey, this blesses them (Heb. 12:11). So it is with God. God disciplines His children when they disobey Him in order to bring them to repentance. The God of love and peace is with His people when they obey Him imperfectly yet sincerely through faith in Christ. Let us obey the God of love and peace and experience His blessing, both personally and in our churches.

Each Person of the Godhead blesses His people, both jointly and distinctly. Paul began with the grace of the Lord Jesus Christ because Christ is the door through which God enters into fellowship with us. Each Person of the Godhead works in giving us grace, but the names ascribed to Christ in this text show why grace is attached to His name in a special way. It is the grace of the Lord. He is the Lord of glory (1 Cor. 2:8), who in His power and might as God, and in His office as King is able to subdue us to Himself, to rule and defend us, and to restrain and conquer all His and our enemies.[78] It is the grace of Jesus. Jesus means, "Jehovah saves." The angel told Joseph, "you shall call His name Jesus, for He shall save His people from their sins" (Matt. 1:21). As our Great High Priest, Jesus offered up Himself as a sacrifice to satisfy divine justice to reconcile us to God. As Priest, He also makes continual intercession for us.[79] It is the grace of Christ. Christ means anointed one. The Father anointed Christ with the Spirit (Acts 10:38) and He received Him without measure (John 3:34). The Father anointed Him with the Spirit in all of His offices. Not only is the Lord Jesus our priest and our king. He is our prophet who reveals to us by His Word and Spirit the will of God for our salvation.[80] Rest in the grace of the Lord Jesus Christ through His threefold office.

The Father represents the love of the entire Godhead. Just as adoption summarizes all of the benefits of the Gospel, so love summarizes the entire work of God in salvation. Behind the grace of the Lord Jesus Christ is the love of God for His people. Trust in the love of God as you come to the Father through the grace of the Lord Jesus Christ.

---

[78] *Westminster Shorter Catechism*, question 26.
[79] *Westminster Shorter Catechism*, question 25.
[80] *Westminster Shorter Catechism*, question 24.

The Spirit is the bond of fellowship between God and our souls. He is the seal of our redemption (2 Cor. 1:22). As we have seen, the sealing of the Holy Spirit is objective. We know that we have the seal of the Spirit when we come to the Father through the Son. Call to mind particularly when you receive this benediction that the Spirit is our down payment of heaven as well (2 Cor. 5:5; Eph. 1:14). This reminds us that God Himself is our portion and our inheritance (Ps. 16:5; Lam. 3:24).

This Triune blessing in this passage comes to us in two ways. First, God blesses His obedient people. Therefore, let us walk by the Sprit so that we do not fulfill the lusts of the flesh (Gal. 5:16). Let us obey the Father's laws that He has revealed in Scripture. Let us love Christ and keep His commandments (John 14:15, 21, 23). Learn to walk daily in fellowship with God by His Word and Spirit and the God of love and peace will be with you (2 Cor. 13:11). Second, God pronounces His blessing upon us through His ministers. When the minister proclaims the benediction from Scripture at the end of the worship service, do not bow your head and close your eyes. Lift up your head towards heaven and expect the blessing of the Triune God with joyful faith.

This chapter forms a fitting conclusion to this book. We need to cultivate Trinitarian faith and a Trinity-dependent Christian life. We must be self-consciously Trinitarian as we understand Christ's person and work, the doctrine of the Church, our exercise of spiritual gifts, and our communion with God in the Word, in prayer, and through the sacraments. The glory of the Triune God is the heart of the Gospel, the focus of Scripture, the meaning of life, and goal of the Christian life. As Edward Leigh (1602–1671) wrote, "We should praise God for revealing this mystery to us in His Word, and be assured that what He promiseth or threatens shall be accomplished, being confirmed by three witnesses."[81] Let us develop a Trinitarian piety.

---

[81] Edward Leigh, *A Systeme or Body of Divinity Consisting of Ten Books, Wherein the Fundamentals and Main Grounds of Religion Are Opened* (London: Printed by A.M. for William Lee, 1662), 215.

Study Questions:

1. What is a benediction? How do benedictions differ from doxologies? Can you think of examples where people confuse these two things?
2. How is godly living related to receiving God's benediction?
3. What do the titles given to Christ in this benediction teach us? How should these things strengthen our confident trust in Christ?
4. Why is Christ likely mentioned first in this benediction?
5. Why is this chapter a fitting conclusion to this book? How does it tie together the themes of all of the preceding chapters? How should we respond?

Appendix: Triadic Passages in Scripture

This book provides a representative sample only of passages in Scripture that mention or allude to all three divine Persons. By providing the list of passages below, I hope to help readers meditate on the glory of the Triune God. Understanding and identifying some of these passages enables us to apply similar principles to other passages. This list is not exhaustive and it does not reflect adequately chapters in Scripture, both in the Old Testament and in the New, where all three Persons appear in a single chapter, though not necessarily in the same verse, as for example in Philippians 1. As you mediate on these passages, keep in mind that the Father originates every divine work, the Son accomplishes it, and the Spirit perfects or completes it. These passages bear out particularly the fact that God saves us from the Father, through the Son, and by the Spirit and that we come to God by the Spirit, through the Son, to the Father.

"In the beginning God created the heavens and the earth. The earth was without form, and void; and darkness was on the face of the deep. And the Spirit of God was hovering over the face of the waters." Genesis 1:1–2

"By the word of the LORD the heavens were made, and all the host of them by the breath of His mouth." Psalm 33:6

"Come near to Me, hear this: I have not spoken in secret from the beginning; from the time that it was, I was there. And now the Lord GOD and His Spirit have sent Me." Isaiah 48:16

"When He had been baptized, Jesus came up immediately from the water; and behold, the heavens were opened to Him, and He saw the Spirit of God descending like a dove and alighting upon Him.

And suddenly a voice came from heaven, saying, 'This is My beloved Son, in whom I am well pleased.'" Matthew 3:16–17

"Then Jesus was led up by the Spirit into the wilderness to be tempted by the devil. And when He had fasted forty days and forty nights, afterward He was hungry. Now when the tempter came to Him, he said, 'If You are the Son of God, command that these stones become bread.'" Matthew 4:1–3

"Behold! My Servant whom I have chosen, My Beloved in whom My soul is well pleased! I will put My Spirit upon Him, and He will declare justice to the Gentiles." Matthew 12:18

"And if I cast out demons by Beelzebub, by whom do your sons cast them out? Therefore they shall be your judges. But if I cast out demons by the Spirit of God, surely the kingdom of God has come upon you." Matthew 12:27–28

"While the Pharisees were gathered together, Jesus asked them, saying, 'What do you think about the Christ? Whose Son is He?' They said to Him, 'The Son of David.' He said to them, 'How then does David in the Spirit call Him "Lord," saying: "The LORD said to my Lord, 'Sit at My right hand, Till I make Your enemies Your footstool'"? If David then calls Him "Lord," how is He his Son?'" Matthew 22:41-45

"And Jesus came and spoke to them, saying, 'All authority has been given to Me in heaven and on earth. Go therefore and make disciples of all the nations, baptizing them in the name of the Father and of the Son and of the Holy Spirit, teaching them to observe all things that I have commanded you; and lo, I am with you always, even to the end of the age.' Amen." Matthew 28:18-20

"It came to pass in those days that Jesus came from Nazareth of Galilee, and was baptized by John in the Jordan. And immediately, coming up from the water, He saw the heavens parting and the Spirit descending upon Him like a dove. Then a voice came from heaven, 'You are My beloved Son, in whom I am well pleased.'" Mark 1:9-11

"Then Jesus answered and said, while He taught in the temple, 'How is it that the scribes say that the Christ is the Son of David? For David himself said by the Holy Spirit: "The LORD said to my Lord, 'Sit at My right hand, till I make Your enemies Your footstool.'" Therefore David himself calls Him "Lord"; how is He then his Son?' And the common people heard Him gladly." Mark 12:35-37

"For he will be great in the sight of the Lord, and shall drink neither wine nor strong drink. He will also be filled with the Holy Spirit, even from his mother's womb. And he will turn many of the children of Israel to the Lord their God." Luke 1:15-16

"And the angel answered and said to her, 'The Holy Spirit will come upon you, and the power of the Highest will overshadow you; therefore, also, that Holy One who is to be born will be called the Son of God.'" Luke 1:35

"And it had been revealed to him by the Holy Spirit that he would not see death before he had seen the Lord's Christ." Luke 2:26

"When all the people were baptized, it came to pass that Jesus also was baptized; and while He prayed, the heaven was opened. And the Holy Spirit descended in bodily form like a dove upon Him, and a voice came from heaven which said, 'You are My beloved Son; in You I am well pleased.'" Luke 3:21-22

"Then Jesus, being filled with the Holy Spirit, returned from the Jordan and was led by the Spirit into the wilderness, being tempted for forty days by the devil. And in those days He ate nothing, and afterward, when they had ended, He was hungry. And the devil said to Him, 'If You are the Son of God, command this stone to become bread.'" Luke 4:1-3

"The Spirit of the LORD is upon Me, Because He has anointed Me To preach the gospel to the poor; He has sent Me to heal the brokenhearted, to proclaim liberty to the captives and recovery of sight to the blind, to set at liberty those who are oppressed; to proclaim the acceptable year of the LORD." Luke 4:18-19

"In that hour Jesus rejoiced in the Spirit and said, 'I thank You, Father, Lord of heaven and earth, that You have hidden these things from the wise and prudent and revealed them to babes. Even so, Father, for so it seemed good in Your sight.'" Luke 10:21

"If you then, being evil, know how to give good gifts to your children, how much more will your heavenly Father give the Holy Spirit to those who ask Him!" Luke 11:13

"Also I say to you, whoever confesses Me before men, him the Son of Man also will confess before the angels of God. But he who denies Me before men will be denied before the angels of God. And anyone who speaks a word against the Son of Man, it will be forgiven him; but to him who blasphemes against the Holy Spirit, it will not be forgiven. Now when they bring you to the synagogues and magistrates and authorities, do not worry about how or what you should answer, or what you should say. For the Holy Spirit will teach you in that very hour what you ought to say." Luke 12:8–12

"And John bore witness, saying, 'I saw the Spirit descending from heaven like a dove, and He remained upon Him. I did not know Him, but He who sent me to baptize with water said to me, "Upon whom you see the Spirit descending, and remaining on Him, this is He who baptizes with the Holy Spirit." And I have seen and testified that this is the Son of God.'" John 1:32–34

"There was a man of the Pharisees named Nicodemus, a ruler of the Jews. This man came to Jesus by night and said to Him, 'Rabbi, we know that You are a teacher come from God; for no one can do these signs that You do unless God is with him.' Jesus answered and said to him, 'Most assuredly, I say to you, unless one is born again, he cannot see the kingdom of God.' Nicodemus said to Him, 'How can a man be born when he is old? Can he enter a second time into his mother's womb and be born?' Jesus answered, 'Most assuredly, I say to you, unless one is born of water and the Spirit, he cannot enter the kingdom of God.'" John 3:1–5

"For He whom God has sent speaks the words of God, for God does not give the Spirit by measure." John 3:34

"God is Spirit, and those who worship Him must worship in spirit and truth." John 4:24

"'It is the Spirit who gives life; the flesh profits nothing. The words that I speak to you are spirit, and they are life. But there are some of you who do not believe.' For Jesus knew from the beginning who they were who did not believe, and who would betray Him. And He said, 'Therefore I have said to you that no one can come to Me unless it has been granted to him by My Father.'" John 6:63–65

"If you love Me, keep My commandments. And I will pray the Father, and He will give you another Helper, that He may abide with you forever – the Spirit of truth, whom the world cannot receive, because it neither sees Him nor knows Him; but you know Him, for He dwells with you and will be in you. I will not leave you orphans; I will come to you." John 14:15–18

"These things I have spoken to you while being present with you. But the Helper, the Holy Spirit, whom the Father will send in My name, He will teach you all things, and bring to your remembrance all things that I said to you." John 14:25-26

"But when the Helper comes, whom I shall send to you from the Father, the Spirit of truth who proceeds from the Father, He will testify of Me. And you also will bear witness, because you have been with Me from the beginning." John 15:26-27

"I still have many things to say to you, but you cannot bear them now. However, when He, the Spirit of truth, has come, He will guide you into all truth; for He will not speak on His own authority, but whatever He hears He will speak; and He will tell you things to come. He will glorify Me, for He will take of what is Mine and declare it to you. All things that the Father has are Mine. Therefore I said that He will take of Mine and declare it to you." John 16:12-15

"So Jesus said to them again, 'Peace to you! As the Father has sent Me, I also send you.' And when He had said this, He breathed on them, and said to them, 'Receive the Holy Spirit. If you forgive the sins of any, they are forgiven them; if you retain the sins of any, they are retained.'" John 20:21-23

"The former account I made, O Theophilus, of all that Jesus began both to do and teach, until the day in which He was taken up, after He through the Holy Spirit had given commandments to the apostles whom He had chosen, to whom He also presented Himself alive after His suffering by many infallible proofs, being seen by them during forty days and speaking of the things pertaining to the kingdom of God." Acts 1:1-3

"And being assembled together with them, He commanded them not to depart from Jerusalem, but to wait for the Promise of the Father, 'which,' He said, 'you have heard from Me; for John truly baptized with water, but you shall be baptized with the Holy Spirit not many days from now.'" Acts 1:4-5

"And it shall come to pass in the last days, says God, That I will pour out of My Spirit on all flesh; Your sons and your daughters shall prophesy, Your young men shall see visions, Your old men shall dream dreams. And on My menservants and on My maidservants I will pour out My Spirit in those days; And they shall prophesy. I will show wonders in heaven above and signs in the earth beneath: Blood and fire and vapor of smoke ... And it shall come to pass that whoever calls on the name of the LORD shall be saved." Acts 2:17-19, 21

"Therefore being exalted to the right hand of God, and having received from the Father the promise of the Holy Spirit, He poured out this which you now see and hear." Acts 2:33

"Then Peter said to them, 'Repent, and let every one of you be baptized in the name of Jesus Christ for the remission of sins; and you shall receive the gift of the Holy Spirit. For the promise is to you and to your children, and to all who are afar off, as many as the Lord our God will call.'" Acts 2:38–39

"Then Peter, filled with the Holy Spirit, said to them, 'Rulers of the people and elders of Israel: If we this day are judged for a good deed done to a helpless man, by what means he has been made well, let it be known to you all, and to all the people of Israel, that by the name of Jesus Christ of Nazareth, whom you crucified, whom God raised from the dead, by Him this man stands here before you whole.'" Acts 4:8–10

"'For truly against Your holy Servant Jesus, whom You anointed, both Herod and Pontius Pilate, with the Gentiles and the people of Israel, were gathered together to do whatever Your hand and Your purpose determined before to be done. Now, Lord, look on their threats, and grant to Your servants that with all boldness they may speak Your word, by stretching out Your hand to heal, and that signs and wonders may be done through the name of Your holy Servant Jesus.' And when they had prayed, the place where they were assembled together was shaken; and they were all filled with the Holy Spirit, and they spoke the word of God with boldness." Acts 4:27–31

"But Peter and the other apostles answered and said: 'We ought to obey God rather than men. The God of our fathers raised up Jesus whom you murdered by hanging on a tree. Him God has exalted to His right hand to be Prince and Savior, to give repentance to Israel and forgiveness of sins. And we are His witnesses to these things, and so also is the Holy Spirit whom God has given to those who obey Him.'" Acts 5:29–32

"But he, being full of the Holy Spirit, gazed into heaven and saw the glory of God, and Jesus standing at the right hand of God, and said, 'Look! I see the heavens opened and the Son of Man standing at the right hand of God!'" Acts 7:55–56

"Now when the apostles who were at Jerusalem heard that Samaria had received the word of God, they sent Peter and John to them, who, when they had come down, prayed for them that they might receive the Holy Spirit. For as yet He had fallen upon none of them. They had only been baptized in the name of the Lord Jesus." Acts 8:14–16

"Then Philip said, 'If you believe with all your heart, you may.' And he answered and said, 'I believe that Jesus Christ is the Son of God.' So he commanded the chariot to stand still. And both Philip and the eunuch went down into the water, and he baptized him. Now when they came up out of the water, the Spirit of the Lord caught Philip away, so that the eunuch saw him no more; and he went on his way rejoicing. But Philip was found at Azotus. And passing through, he preached in all the cities till he came to Caesarea." Acts 8:37–40

"The word which God sent to the children of Israel, preaching peace through Jesus Christ— He is Lord of all— that word you know, which was proclaimed throughout all Judea, and began from Galilee after the baptism which John preached: how God anointed Jesus of Nazareth with the Holy Spirit and with power, who went about doing good and healing all who were oppressed by the devil, for God was with Him." Acts 10:36–38

"While Peter was still speaking these words, the Holy Spirit fell upon all those who heard the word. And those of the circumcision who believed were astonished, as many as came with Peter, because the gift of the Holy Spirit had been poured out on the Gentiles also. For they heard them speak with tongues and magnify God. Then Peter answered, 'Can anyone forbid water, that these should not be baptized who have received the Holy Spirit just as we have?' And he commanded them to be baptized in the name of the Lord. Then they asked him to stay a few days." Acts 10:44–48

"And as I began to speak, the Holy Spirit fell upon them, as upon us at the beginning. Then I remembered the word of the Lord, how He said, 'John indeed baptized with water, but you shall be baptized with the Holy Spirit.' If therefore God gave them the same gift as He gave us when we believed on the Lord Jesus Christ, who was I that I could withstand God?" Acts 11:15–17

"Then news of these things came to the ears of the church in Jerusalem, and they sent out Barnabas to go as far as Antioch. When he came and had seen the grace of God, he was glad, and encouraged them all that with purpose of heart they should continue with the Lord. For he was a good man, full of the Holy Spirit and of faith. And a great many people were added to the Lord." Acts 11:22–24

"When Silas and Timothy had come from Macedonia, Paul was compelled by the Spirit, and testified to the Jews that Jesus is the Christ. But when they opposed him and blasphemed, he shook his garments and said to them, 'Your blood be upon your own heads; I am clean. From now on I will go to the Gentiles.' And he departed from there and entered the house of a certain man named Justus, one who worshiped God, whose house was next door to the synagogue. Then Crispus, the ruler of the synagogue, believed on the Lord with all his household. And many of the Corinthians, hearing, believed and were baptized." Acts 18:5–8

"Testifying to Jews, and also to Greeks, repentance toward God and faith toward our Lord Jesus Christ. And see, now I go bound in the spirit to Jerusalem, not knowing the things that will happen to me there, except that the Holy Spirit testifies in every city, saying that chains and tribulations await me." Acts 20:21–23

"Therefore take heed to yourselves and to all the flock, among which the Holy Spirit has made you overseers, to shepherd the church of God which He purchased with His own blood." Acts 20:28

"So when they did not agree among themselves, they departed after Paul had said one word: 'The Holy Spirit spoke rightly through Isaiah the prophet to our fathers, saying, "Go to this people and say: 'Hearing you will hear, and shall not understand; and seeing you will see, and not perceive; for the hearts of this people have grown dull. Their ears are hard of hearing, and their eyes they have closed, lest they should see with their eyes and hear with their ears, lest they should understand with their hearts and turn, so that I should heal them.'" Therefore let it be known to you that the salvation of God has been sent to the Gentiles, and they will hear it!' And when he had said these words, the Jews departed and had a great dispute among themselves. Then Paul dwelt two whole years in his own rented house, and received all who came to him, preaching the kingdom of God and teaching the things which concern the Lord Jesus Christ with all confidence, no one forbidding him." Acts 28:25–31

"Paul, a bondservant of Jesus Christ, called to be an apostle, separated to the gospel of God which He promised before through His prophets in the Holy Scriptures, concerning His Son Jesus Christ our Lord, who was born of the seed of David according to the flesh, and declared to be the Son of God with power according to the Spirit of holiness, by the resurrection from the dead." Romans 1:1–4

"Therefore, having been justified by faith, we have peace with God through our Lord Jesus Christ, through whom also we have access by faith into this grace in which we stand, and rejoice in hope of the glory of God. And not only that, but we also glory in tribulations, knowing that tribulation produces perseverance; and perseverance, character; and character, hope. Now hope does not disappoint, because the love of God has been poured out in our hearts by the Holy Spirit who was given to us." Romans 5:1–5

"There is therefore now no condemnation to those who are in Christ Jesus, who do not walk according to the flesh, but according to the Spirit. For the law of the Spirit of life in Christ Jesus has made me free from the law of sin and death. For what the law could not do in that it was weak through the flesh, God did by sending His own Son in the likeness of sinful flesh, on account of sin: He condemned sin in the flesh, that the righteous requirement of the law might be fulfilled in us who do not walk according to the flesh but according to the Spirit." Romans 8:1–4

"But you are not in the flesh but in the Spirit, if indeed the Spirit of God dwells in you. Now if anyone does not have the Spirit of Christ, he is not His. And if Christ is in you, the body is dead because of sin, but the Spirit is life because of righteousness. But if the Spirit of Him who raised Jesus from the dead dwells in you, He who raised Christ from the dead will also give life to your mortal bodies through His Spirit who dwells in you." Romans 8:9-11

"The Spirit Himself bears witness with our spirit that we are children of God, and if children, then heirs—heirs of God and joint heirs with Christ, if indeed we suffer with Him, that we may also be glorified together." Romans 8:16–17

"I tell the truth in Christ, I am not lying, my conscience also bearing me witness in the Holy Spirit, that I have great sorrow and continual grief in my heart. For I could wish that I myself were accursed from Christ for my brethren, my countrymen according to the flesh, who are Israelites, to whom pertain the adoption, the glory, the covenants, the giving of the law, the service of God, and the promises; of whom are the fathers and from whom, according to the flesh, Christ came, who is over all, the eternally blessed God. Amen." Romans 9:1–5

"Nevertheless, brethren, I have written more boldly to you on some points, as reminding you, because of the grace given to me by God, that I might be a minister of Jesus Christ to the Gentiles, ministering the gospel of God, that the offering of the Gentiles might be acceptable, sanctified by the Holy Spirit. Therefore I have reason to glory in Christ Jesus in the things which pertain to God. For I will not dare to speak of any of those things which Christ has not accomplished through me, in word and deed, to make the Gentiles obedient—in mighty signs and wonders, by the power of the Spirit of God, so that from Jerusalem and round about to Illyricum I have fully preached the gospel of Christ. And so I have made it my aim to preach the gospel, not where Christ was named, lest I should build on another man's foundation." Romans 15:15–20

"Now I beg you, brethren, through the Lord Jesus Christ, and through the love of the Spirit, that you strive together with me in prayers to God for me, that I may be delivered from those in Judea who do not believe, and that my service for Jerusalem may be acceptable to the saints, that I may come to you with joy by the will of God, and may be refreshed together with you. Now the God of peace be with you all. Amen." Romans 15:30–33

"And I, brethren, when I came to you, did not come with excellence of speech or of wisdom declaring to you the testimony of God. For I determined not to know anything among you except Jesus Christ and Him crucified. I was with you in weakness, in fear, and in much trembling. And my speech and my preaching were not with persuasive words of human wisdom, but in demonstration of the Spirit and of power, that your faith should not be in the wisdom of men but in the power of God." 1 Corinthians 2:1–5

"Do you not know that you are the temple of God and that the Spirit of God dwells in you? If anyone defiles the temple of God, God will destroy him. For the temple of God is holy, which temple you are [...] And you are Christ's, and Christ is God's." 1 Corinthians 3:16–17, 23

"Do you not know that the unrighteous will not inherit the kingdom of God? Do not be deceived. Neither fornicators, nor idolaters, nor adulterers, nor homosexuals, nor sodomites, nor thieves, nor covetous, nor drunkards, nor revilers, nor extortioners will inherit the kingdom of God. And such were some of you. But you were washed, but you were sanctified, but you were justified in the name of the Lord Jesus and by the Spirit of our God." 1 Corinthians 6:9–11

"Or do you not know that your body is the temple of the Holy Spirit who is in you, whom you have from God, and you are not your own? For you were bought at a price; therefore glorify God in your body and in your spirit, which are God's." 1 Corinthians 6:19–20

"Therefore I make known to you that no one speaking by the Spirit of God calls Jesus accursed, and no one can say that Jesus is Lord except by the Holy Spirit." 1 Corinthians 12:3

"There are diversities of gifts, but the same Spirit. There are differences of ministries, but the same Lord. And there are diversities of activities, but it is the same God who works all in all. But the manifestation of the Spirit is given to each one for the profit of all." 1 Corinthians 12:4–7

"Blessed be the God and Father of our Lord Jesus Christ, the Father of mercies and God of all comfort, who comforts us in all our tribulation, that we may be able to comfort those who are in any trouble, with the comfort with which we ourselves are comforted by God. For as the sufferings of Christ abound in us, so our consolation also abounds through Christ [...] For all the promises of God in Him are Yes, and in Him Amen, to the glory of God through us. Now He who establishes us with you in Christ and has anointed us is God, who also has sealed us and given us the Spirit in our hearts as a guarantee." 2 Corinthians 1:3-5, 20-22

"And we have such trust through Christ toward God. Not that we are sufficient of ourselves to think of anything as being from ourselves, but our sufficiency is from God, who also made us sufficient as ministers of the new covenant, not of the letter but of the Spirit; for the letter kills, but the Spirit gives life." 2 Corinthians 3:4-6

"The grace of the Lord Jesus Christ, and the love of God, and the communion of the Holy Spirit be with you all. Amen." 2 Corinthians 13:14

"O foolish Galatians! Who has bewitched you that you should not obey the truth, before whose eyes Jesus Christ was clearly portrayed among you as crucified? This only I want to learn from you: Did you receive the Spirit by the works of the law, or by the hearing of faith? Are you so foolish? Having begun in the Spirit, are you now being made perfect by the flesh? Have you suffered so many things in vain—if indeed it was in vain? Therefore He who supplies the Spirit to you and works miracles among you, does He do it by the works of the law, or by the hearing of faith?—just as Abraham 'believed God, and it was accounted to him for righteousness.' Therefore know that only those who are of faith are sons of Abraham." Galatians 3:1-7

"And because you are sons, God has sent forth the Spirit of His Son into your hearts, crying out, 'Abba, Father!' Therefore you are no longer a slave but a son, and if a son, then an heir of God through Christ." Galatians 4:6-7

"[...] envy, murders, drunkenness, revelries, and the like; of which I tell you beforehand, just as I also told you in time past, that those who practice such things will not inherit the kingdom of God. But the fruit of the Spirit is love, joy, peace, longsuffering, kindness, goodness, faithfulness, gentleness, self-control. Against such there is no law. And those who are Christ's have crucified the flesh with its passions and desires. If we live in the Spirit, let us also walk in the Spirit. Let us not become conceited, provoking one another, envying one another." Galatians 5:21-26

"Blessed be the God and Father of our Lord Jesus Christ, who has blessed us with every spiritual blessing in the heavenly places in Christ, just as He chose us in Him before the foundation of the world, that we should be holy and without blame before Him in love, having predestined us to adoption as sons by Jesus Christ to Himself, according to the good pleasure of His will, to the praise of the glory of His grace, by which He made us accepted in the Beloved. In Him we have redemption through His blood, the forgiveness of sins, according to the riches of His grace which He made to abound toward us in all wisdom and prudence, having made known to us the mystery of His will, according to His good pleasure which He purposed in Himself, that in the dispensation of the fullness of the times He might gather together in one all things in Christ, both which are in heaven and which are on earth—in Him. In Him also we have obtained an inheritance, being predestined according to the purpose of Him who works all things according to the counsel of His will, that we who first trusted in Christ should be to the praise of His glory. In Him you also trusted, after you heard the word of truth, the gospel of your salvation; in whom also, having believed, you were sealed with the Holy Spirit of promise, who is the guarantee of our inheritance until the redemption of the purchased possession, to the praise of His glory." Ephesians 1:3-14

"For through Him we both have access by one Spirit to the Father." Ephesians 2:18

"Now, therefore, you are no longer strangers and foreigners, but fellow citizens with the saints and members of the household of God, having been built on the foundation of the apostles and prophets, Jesus Christ Himself being the chief corner stone, in whom the whole building, being fitted together, grows into a holy temple in the Lord, in whom you also are being built together for a dwelling place of God in the Spirit." Ephesians 2:19–22

"which in other ages was not made known to the sons of men, as it has now been revealed by the Spirit to His holy apostles and prophets: that the Gentiles should be fellow heirs, of the same body, and partakers of His promise in Christ through the gospel, of which I became a minister according to the gift of the grace of God given to me by the effective working of His power." Ephesians 3:5–7

"For this reason I bow my knees to the Father of our Lord Jesus Christ, from whom the whole family in heaven and earth is named, that He would grant you, according to the riches of His glory, to be strengthened with might through His Spirit in the inner man, that Christ may dwell in your hearts through faith; that you, being rooted and grounded in love, may be able to comprehend with all the saints what is the width and length and depth and height— to know the love of Christ which passes knowledge; that you may be filled with all the fullness of God." Ephesians 3:14–19

"There is one body and one Spirit, just as you were called in one hope of your calling; one Lord, one faith, one baptism; one God and Father of all, who is above all, and through all, and in you all." Ephesians 4:4–6

"And do not grieve the Holy Spirit of God, by whom you were sealed for the day of redemption. Let all bitterness, wrath, anger, clamor, and evil speaking be put away from you, with all malice. And be kind to one another, tenderhearted, forgiving one another, even as God in Christ forgave you." Ephesians 4:30–32

"And do not be drunk with wine, in which is dissipation; but be filled with the Spirit, speaking to one another in psalms and hymns and spiritual songs, singing and making melody in your heart to the Lord, giving thanks always for all things to God the Father in the name of our Lord Jesus Christ, submitting to one another in the fear of God." Ephesians 5:18–21

"Therefore if there is any consolation in Christ, if any comfort of love, if any fellowship of the Spirit, if any affection and mercy, fulfill my joy by being like-minded, having the same love, being of one accord, of one mind [...] Let this mind be in you which was also in Christ Jesus, who, being in the form of God, did not consider it robbery to be equal with God," Philippians 2:1–2, 5–6

"For we are the circumcision, who worship God in the Spirit, rejoice in Christ Jesus, and have no confidence in the flesh," Philippians 3:3

"We give thanks to the God and Father of our Lord Jesus Christ, praying always for you, since we heard of your faith in Christ Jesus and of your love for all the saints [...] who also declared to us your love in the Spirit." Colossians 1:3–4, 8

"We give thanks to God always for you all, making mention of you in our prayers, remembering without ceasing your work of faith, labor of love, and patience of hope in our Lord Jesus Christ in the sight of our God and Father, knowing, beloved brethren, your election by God. For our gospel did not come to you in word only, but also in power, and in the Holy Spirit and in much assurance, as you know what kind of men we were among you for your sake." 1 Thessalonians 1:2–5

"And you became followers of us and of the Lord, having received the word in much affliction, with joy of the Holy Spirit, so that you became examples to all in Macedonia and Achaia who believe. For from you the word of the Lord has sounded forth, not only in Macedonia and Achaia, but also in every place. Your faith toward God has gone out, so that we do not need to say anything." 1 Thessalonians1:6–8

"Do not quench the Spirit. Do not despise prophecies. Test all things; hold fast what is good. Abstain from every form of evil. Now may the God of peace Himself sanctify you completely; and may your whole spirit, soul, and body be preserved blameless at the coming of our Lord Jesus Christ. He who calls you is faithful, who also will do it." 1 Thessalonians 5:19–24

"But we are bound to give thanks to God always for you, brethren beloved by the Lord, because God from the beginning chose you for salvation through sanctification by the Spirit and belief in the truth, to which He called you by our gospel, for the obtaining of the glory of our Lord Jesus Christ. Therefore, brethren, stand fast and hold the traditions which you were taught, whether by word or our epistle." 2 Thessalonians 2:13–15

"These things I write to you, though I hope to come to you shortly; but if I am delayed, I write so that you may know how you ought to conduct yourself in the house of God, which is the church of the living God, the pillar and ground of the truth. And without controversy great is the mystery of godliness: God was manifested in the flesh, Justified in the Spirit, Seen by angels, Preached among the Gentiles, Believed on in the world, Received up in glory." 1 Timothy 3:14–16

"Now the Spirit expressly says that in latter times some will depart from the faith, giving heed to deceiving spirits and doctrines of demons, speaking lies in hypocrisy, having their own conscience seared with a hot iron, forbidding to marry, and commanding to abstain from foods which God created to be received with thanksgiving by those who believe and know the truth. For every creature of God is good, and nothing is to be refused if it is received with thanksgiving; for it is sanctified by the word of God and prayer. If you instruct the brethren in these things, you will be a good minister of Jesus Christ, nourished in the words of faith and of the good doctrine which you have carefully followed." 1 Timothy 4:1–6

"Therefore do not be ashamed of the testimony of our Lord, nor of me His prisoner, but share with me in the sufferings for the gospel according to the power of God, who has saved us and called us with a holy calling, not according to our works, but according to His own purpose and grace which was given to us in Christ Jesus before time began, but has now been revealed by the appearing of our Savior Jesus Christ, who has abolished death and brought life and immortality to light through the gospel, to which I was appointed a preacher, an apostle, and a teacher of the Gentiles. For this reason I also suffer these things; nevertheless I am not ashamed, for I know whom I have believed and am persuaded that He is able to keep what I have committed to Him until that Day. Hold fast the pattern of sound words which you have heard from me, in faith and love which are in Christ Jesus. That good thing which was committed to you, keep by the Holy Spirit who dwells in us." 2 Timothy 1:8–14

"But when the kindness and the love of God our Savior toward man appeared, not by works of righteousness which we have done, but according to His mercy He saved us, through the washing of regeneration and renewing of the Holy Spirit, whom He poured out on us abundantly through Jesus Christ our Savior, that having been justified by His grace we should become heirs according to the hope of eternal life." Titus 3:4–7

"Therefore we must give the more earnest heed to the things we have heard, lest we drift away. For if the word spoken through angels proved steadfast, and every transgression and disobedience received a just reward, how shall we escape if we neglect so great a salvation, which at the first began to be spoken by the Lord, and was confirmed to us by those who heard Him, God also bearing witness both with signs and wonders, with various miracles, and gifts of the Holy Spirit, according to His own will?" Hebrews 2:1–4

"For every house is built by someone, but He who built all things is God. And Moses indeed was faithful in all His house as a servant, for a testimony of those things which would be spoken afterward, but Christ as a Son over His own house, whose house we are if we hold fast the confidence and the rejoicing of the hope firm to the end. Therefore, as the Holy Spirit says: 'Today, if you will hear His voice,'" Hebrews 3:4–7

"For it is impossible for those who were once enlightened, and have tasted the heavenly gift, and have become partakers of the Holy Spirit, and have tasted the good word of God and the powers of the age to come, if they fall away, to renew them again to repentance, since they crucify again for themselves the Son of God, and put Him to an open shame." Hebrews 6:4–6

"For if the blood of bulls and goats and the ashes of a heifer, sprinkling the unclean, sanctifies for the purifying of the flesh, how much more shall the blood of Christ, who through the eternal Spirit offered Himself without spot to God, cleanse your conscience from dead works to serve the living God?" Hebrews 9:13–14

"But this Man, after He had offered one sacrifice for sins forever, sat down at the right hand of God, from that time waiting till His enemies are made His footstool. For by one offering He has perfected forever those who are being sanctified. But the Holy Spirit also witnesses to us; for after He had said before," Hebrews 10:12–15

"Peter, an apostle of Jesus Christ, To the pilgrims of the Dispersion in Pontus, Galatia, Cappadocia, Asia, and Bithynia, elect according to the foreknowledge of God the Father, in sanctification of the Spirit, for obedience and sprinkling of the blood of Jesus Christ: Grace to you and peace be multiplied." 1 Peter 1:1–2

"Of this salvation the prophets have inquired and searched carefully, who prophesied of the grace that would come to you, searching what, or what manner of time, the Spirit of Christ who was in them was indicating when He testified beforehand the sufferings of Christ and the glories that would follow. To them it was revealed that, not to themselves, but to us they were ministering the things which now have been reported to you through those who have preached the gospel to you by the Holy Spirit sent from heaven—things which angels desire to look into. Therefore gird up the loins of your mind, be sober, and rest your hope fully upon the grace that is to be brought to you at the revelation of Jesus Christ; as obedient children, not conforming yourselves to the former lusts, as in your ignorance; but as He who called you is holy, you also be holy in all your conduct, because it is written, 'Be holy, for I am holy.' And if you call on the Father, who without partiality judges according to each one's work, conduct yourselves throughout the time of your stay here in fear;" 1 Peter 1:10-17

"Coming to Him as to a living stone, rejected indeed by men, but chosen by God and precious, you also, as living stones, are being built up a spiritual house, a holy priesthood, to offer up spiritual sacrifices acceptable to God through Jesus Christ." 1 Peter 2:4-5

"For Christ also suffered once for sins, the just for the unjust, that He might bring us to God, being put to death in the flesh but made alive by the Spirit," 1 Peter 3:18

"If you are reproached for the name of Christ, blessed are you, for the Spirit of glory and of God rests upon you. On their part He is blasphemed, but on your part He is glorified." 1 Peter 4:14

"For He received from God the Father honor and glory when such a voice came to Him from the Excellent Glory: "This is My beloved Son, in whom I am well pleased [...] for prophecy never came by the will of man, but holy men of God spoke as they were moved by the Holy Spirit." 2 Peter 1:17, 21

"But you have an anointing from the Holy One, and you know all things. I have not written to you because you do not know the truth, but because you know it, and that no lie is of the truth. Who is a liar but he who denies that Jesus is the Christ? He is antichrist who denies the Father and the Son. Whoever denies the Son does not have the Father either; he who acknowledges the Son has the Father also." 1 John 2:20-23

"Beloved, do not believe every spirit, but test the spirits, whether they are of God; because many false prophets have gone out into the world. By this you know the Spirit of God: Every spirit that confesses that Jesus Christ has come in the flesh is of God, and every spirit that does not confess that Jesus Christ has come in the flesh is not of God. And this is the spirit of the Antichrist, which you have heard was coming, and is now already in the world." 1 John 4:1-3

"By this we know that we abide in Him, and He in us, because He has given us of His Spirit. And we have seen and testify that the Father has sent the Son as Savior of the world." 1 John 4:13-14

"But you, beloved, building yourselves up on your most holy faith, praying in the Holy Spirit, keep yourselves in the love of God, looking for the mercy of our Lord Jesus Christ unto eternal life." Jude 1:20–21

"John, to the seven churches which are in Asia: Grace to you and peace from Him who is and who was and who is to come, and from the seven Spirits who are before His throne, and from Jesus Christ, the faithful witness, the firstborn from the dead, and the ruler over the kings of the earth. To Him who loved us and washed us from our sins in His own blood, and has made us kings and priests to His God and Father, to Him be glory and dominion forever and ever. Amen." Revelation 1:4–6

"I, John, both your brother and companion in the tribulation and kingdom and patience of Jesus Christ, was on the island that is called Patmos for the word of God and for the testimony of Jesus Christ. I was in the Spirit on the Lord's Day, and I heard behind me a loud voice, as of a trumpet," Revelation 1:9–10

"He who has an ear, let him hear what the Spirit says to the churches. To him who overcomes I will give to eat from the tree of life, which is in the midst of the Paradise of God." Revelation 2:7

"And to the angel of the church in Sardis write, 'These things says He who has the seven Spirits of God and the seven stars: "I know your works, that you have a name that you are alive, but you are dead. Be watchful, and strengthen the things which remain, that are ready to die, for I have not found your works perfect before God."'" Revelation 3:1–2

"To him who overcomes I will grant to sit with Me on My throne, as I also overcame and sat down with My Father on His throne. He who has an ear, let him hear what the Spirit says to the churches." Revelation 3:21–22

"And I looked, and behold, in the midst of the throne and of the four living creatures, and in the midst of the elders, stood a Lamb as though it had been slain, having seven horns and seven eyes, which are the seven Spirits of God sent out into all the earth. Then He came and took the scroll out of the right hand of Him who sat on the throne." Revelation 5:6–7

"Here is the patience of the saints; here are those who keep the commandments of God and the faith of Jesus. Then I heard a voice from heaven saying to me, 'Write: "Blessed are the dead who die in the Lord from now on."' 'Yes,' says the Spirit, 'that they may rest from their labors, and their works follow them.'" Revelation 14:12–13

"Then one of the seven angels who had the seven bowls filled with the seven last plagues came to me and talked with me, saying, 'Come, I will show you the bride, the Lamb's wife.' And he carried me away in the Spirit to a great and high mountain, and showed me the great city, the holy Jerusalem, descending out of heaven from God, having the glory of God. Her light was like a most precious stone, like a jasper stone, clear as crystal." Revelation 21:9–11

"'I, Jesus, have sent My angel to testify to you these things in the churches. I am the Root and the Offspring of David, the Bright and Morning Star.' And the Spirit and the bride say, 'Come!' And let him who hears say, 'Come!' And let him who thirsts come. Whoever desires, let him take the water of life freely. For I testify to everyone who hears the words of the prophecy of this book: If anyone adds to these things, God will add to him the plagues that are written in this book; and if anyone takes away from the words of the book of this prophecy, God shall take away his part from the Book of Life, from the holy city, and from the things which are written in this book. He who testifies to these things says, 'Surely I am coming quickly.' Amen. Even so, come, Lord Jesus! The grace of our Lord Jesus Christ be with you all. Amen." Revelation 22:16-21

Bibliography

Bannerman, James. *The Church of Christ: A Treatise on the Nature, Powers, Ordinances, Discipline, and Government of the Christian Church*. Birmingham, AL: Solid Ground Christian Books, 2009.

Burroughs, Jeremiah. *Gospel-Worship, Or, the Right Manner of Sanctifying the Name of God in General and Particularly in These Three Great Ordinances, Viz. 1. Hearing of the Word, 2. Receiving the Lords Supper, 3. Prayer.* London: Printed by Peter Cole, 1658.

Chantry, Walter J. *Signs of the Apostles: Observations on Pentecostalism Old and New*. Edinburgh; Carlisle, Pa.: Banner of Truth Trust, 1976.

Charnock, Stephen. *Several Discourses Upon the Existence and Attributes of God by That Late Eminent Minister of Christ, Mr. Stephen Charnocke, B.d. and Sometimes Fellow of New-Colledge in Oxon*. London: Printed for D. Newman, T. Cockerill, Benj. Griffin, T. Simmons, and Benj. Alsop. And are to be sold by Michael Hide Bookseller in Exon, 1682.

Cheynell, Francis. *The Divine Trinunity of the Father, Son, and Holy Spirit, Or, the Blessed Doctrine of the Three Coessentiall Subsistents in the Eternall Godhead Without Any Confusion or Division of the Distinct Subsistences or Multiplication of the Most Single and Entire Godhead Acknowledged, Beleeved, Adored by Christians, in Opposition to Pagans, Jewes, Mahumetans, Blasphemous and Antichristian Hereticks, Who Say They Are Christians, but Are Not*. London: Printed by T.R. and E.M. for Samuel Gellibrand ..., 1650.

Durham, James. *A Commentarie Upon the Book of the Revelation Wherein the Text Is Explained, the Series of the Several Prophecies Contained in That*

Book, Deduced ...the Periods and Succession of Times At, or About Which, These Prophecies ... Began to Be ... and Those That Are yet to Be Fulfilled ...: Together with Some Practical Observations, and Several Digressions ...: Delivered in Several Lectures. London: Printed for the Company of Stationers, 1658.

Fesko, J. V. *Word, Water, and Spirit: A Reformed Perspective on Baptism*. Grand Rapids, Mich.: Reformation Heritage Books, 2010.

Gaffin, Richard B. *Perspectives on Pentecost: Studies in New Testament Teaching on the Gifts of the Holy Spirit*. Phillipsburg, N.J.: Presbyterian and Reformed Pub. Co., 1979.

Genderen, J. van, and W. H Velema. *Concise Reformed Dogmatics. Edited by Gerrit Bilkes and Ed M Van der Maas*. Phillipsburg, N.J.: P & R Pub., 2008.

Gillespie, Patrick. *The Ark of the Covenant Opened, Or, a Treatise of the Covenant of Redemption Between God and Christ, as the Foundation of the Covenant of Grace the Second Part, Wherein Is Proved, That There Is Such a Covenant, the Necessity of It, the Nature, Properties, Parties Thereof, the Tenor, Articles, Subject-Matter of Redemption, the Commands, Conditions, and Promises Annexed, the Harmony of the Covenant of Reconciliation Made with Sinners, Wherein They Agree, Wherein They Differ, Grounds of Comfort from the Covenant of Suretiship*. London: Printed for Thomas Pankhurst, 1677.

Jones, Mark. *Knowing Christ*. Edinburgh: Banner of Truth, 2015.

Leigh, Edward. *A Systeme or Body of Divinity Consisting of Ten Books, Wherein the Fundamentals and Main Grounds of Religion Are Opened*. London: Printed by A.M. for William Lee, 1662.

Letham, Robert. *The Holy Trinity: In Scripture, History, Theology, and Worship*. Phillipsburg, NJ: P & R Pub., 2004.

Manton, Thomas. *The Complete Works*. London: Nisbet, 1870.

Mastricht, Peter van. *Theoretico-Practica Theologia. Qua, Per Singula Capita Theologica, Pars Exegetica, Dogmatica, Elenchtica & Practica, Perpetua Successione Conjugantur*. Trajecti ad Rhenum, & Amstelodami: Sumptibus Societatis, 1715.

McGraw, Ryan M. *How Do Preaching and Corporate Prayer Work Together?. Cultivating Biblical Godliness*. Grand Rapids, MI: Reformation Heritage Books, 2014.

McGraw, Ryan M. *The Day of Worship: Reassessing the Christian Life in Light of the Sabbath*. Grand Rapids, MI: Reformation Heritage Books, 2011.

McGraw, Ryan M. "*The Need for a Trinitarian Piety (Eph. 2:18)*." In *The Beauty and Glory of the Father*, edited by Joel R. Beeke, 141–53. Grand Rapids: Reformation Heritage Books, 2013.

———. "*The Trinity and Christ's Resurrection*." New Horizons, April 2015, 3–5.

———. *Why Should I Deny Myself?. Cultivating Biblical Godliness*. Grand Rapids, MI: Reformation Heritage Books, 2015.

McGraw, Ryan M., and Ryan Speck. *Is Church Membership Biblical?*. Grand Rapids, MI: Reformation Heritage Books, 2016.

Muller, Richard A. *Dictionary of Latin and Greek Theological Terms: Drawn Principally from Protestant Scholastic Theology*. Grand Rapids, MI: Baker Book House, 1985.

O'Brien, Peter Thomas. *The Letter to the Ephesians*. Grand Rapids, MI: W.B. Eerdmans Publishing Company, 1999.

Owen, John. *The Works of John Owen*, D.D. Edited by William H. Goold. 24 vols. Edinburgh: Johnstone & Hunter, 1850.

Perkins, William. *A Warning Against the Idolatrie of the Last Times and an Instruction Touching Religious, or Diuine Worship*. [Cambridge]: Printed by Iohn Legat, printer to the Vniuersitie of Cambridge. And are to be sold at the signe of the Crowne in Pauls Churchyard [, London], by Simon Waterson, 1601.

Robertson, O. Palmer. *The Final Word: A Biblical Response to the Case for Tongues and Prophecy Today*. Edinburgh: Banner of Truth, 1993.

Sibbes, Richard. *The Complete Works of Richard Sibbes*. 7 vols. Edinburgh: James Nichols, 1862.

Turretin, Francis. *Institutes of Elenctic Theology*. Edited by James T Dennison. Translated by George Musgrave Giger. 3 vols. Phillipsburg, N.J.: P&R Publishing, 1992.

Watson, Thomas. *A Body of Practical Divinity, Consisting of Above One Hundred Seventy Six Sermons on the Lesser Catechism Composed by the Reverend Assembly of Divines at Westminster: With a Supplement of Some Sermons on Several Texts of Scripture. by Thomas Watson, Formerly Minister at St. Stephen's Walbrook, London. Printed from His Own Hand-Writing. Recommended by Several Ministers to Masters of Families and Others*. London: printed for Thomas Parkurst, at the Bible and Three Crowns in Cheapside, near Mercers-Chappel, 1692.

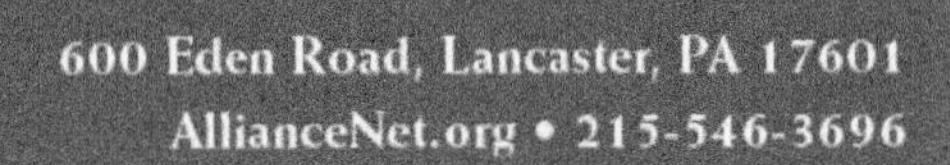

PUBLISHING

reformation21

reformation21 *A Reformed perspective on current issues, grounding readers in the Word of God as proclaimed through the centuries.* Providing an authoritative, Reformed perspective on historic matters and current issues to inform, inspire, and challenge Christians. reformation21.org

Meet the Puritans *Where the dead still speak.* Sharing the theology and piety of the Puritans to reconnect Reformed Christians with their heritage, introduce evangelical Christians to this heritage, and give the world the answers this heritage provides. MeetthePuritans.org

Place for Truth *Exploring the depths of what we believe.* Thoughtful yet accessible biblical, systematic, and practical theology, as well as church history exploring the importance and relevancy of what we believe. PlaceforTruth.org

Daily Devotionals from James Boice and Matthew Henry sent daily to complement your time in the Word. ThinkandActBiblically.org and MatthewHenry.org

Reformed Resources 70 *Years of Reformed Resources.* Thousands of audio on both CD and MP3, video, book, booklet, and e-book resources from trustworthy authors and Alliance speakers. ReformedResources.org

EVENTS

Philadelphia Conference on Reformed Theology and Regional Events *Sound doctrine, boldly preached.* The oldest, continual, national Reformed conference in North America, and regional events including theology and Bible conferences. ReformedEvents.org

Reformation Societies *Encouraging, Emboldening, and Equipping.* Encouraging, emboldening, and equipping pastors and church leaders for the work of biblical reformation in the church. ReformationSocieties.org

The Alliance of Confessing Evangelicals is a coalition of pastors, cholars, and churchmen who hold the historic creeds and confessions of the Reformed faith and who proclaim biblical doctrine in order to foster a Reformed awakening in today's Church.

ALLIANCE
OF CONFESSING EVANGELICALS

600 Eden Road · Lancaster, PA 17601
215-546-3696 · (fax) 215-735-5133
AllianceNet.org

Made in the USA
Las Vegas, NV
17 January 2022